1

THE *CONTEXT* of RESIDENTIAL TREATMENT

A FICTITIOUS (BUT TYPICAL) EXAMPLE

Charlie is 12 years old. He has been apparently well-adjusted and has presented only those periods of difficult behavior that might be expected from a developing, active child. His behavior problem develops gradually, beginning with his defying his parents' directions and replying to them with "smart" but abusive remarks. His behavior becomes more serious in the face of his parents' increasing bewilderment and concern, as his parents try every strategy they know — shouting, threatening, diverting his attention, sending him to his room, hitting, and so on. The busy nature of family life means that their strategies are often not followed through. The more they attempt their solutions, and the more exasperated they become, the more Charlie's behavior persists. After some time, he is having temper tantrums, which involve shouting, throwing objects, and hurling verbal abuse. His parents find this behavior inexplicable, and its effects on the family are becoming worse. They fear the consequences of asking Charlie to do even the smallest household task, since his outbursts seem to be increasing in frequency as both their patience and their sense of competence decrease. Preoccupied with the problem, they have less patience or time for their other children, and they begin to wonder if Charlie is trying to ruin the family.

In sheer frustration, they consult a counselor. "We are having a problem with Charlie. He seems to be having problems with anger. We don't know where it came from, maybe he has low self-esteem, or maybe he is hyperactive. There must be some reason. But we cannot cope, we don't know what to do." No matter how sympathetic the counselor may be, such a conversation is tantamount to saying, "We fear that we are failures as parents."

The counselor offers various pieces of advice. She suggests strategies for managing this behavior and seems somewhat taken aback at the protestations of "We tried that," or "That wouldn't work because. . . ." The parents' feelings of failure mean that they are unlikely to see these suggestions as helpful, and they have little alternative but to strengthen their belief that Charlie has developed some serious pathology.

Finally, after weeks of achieving nothing, they call again. "It's no use. You'll have to arrange a residential placement for Charlie so someone can do something about this problem. We don't know what else to do." Being parents is one thing we are all expected to know how to do—and no one tells us how to do it unless they think we are doing it wrong! These parents might just as well have said, "We need someone to do for us what we have failed to do with our own child," and the very fact of Charlie going off to the residential facility for "intensive treatment" confirms their view of themselves as failures, or their view of him as disturbed, or both. They feel sad driving him there; he appears upset and hesitant, and they leave as quickly as possible. After all, what else could they do?

Once they arrive home, the house is peaceful. They can enjoy a cup of coffee without having to keep watch for Charlie's latest tactic. They can spend time with their daughters. The house is quiet, and it is, in one way, a relief that he has gone. They feel guilty about feeling this; however, there is no denying that the situation is more peaceful. Some might conclude that they had harbored a secret or unconscious rejection of their son, but it is simply that peace and quiet is enjoyable (and further confirms the idea that he was the problem).

After a few weeks (during which they have maintained an interest in Charlie's progress, visited regularly, and delivered clean clothes when necessary), on hearing reports of his having settled down, they begin to worry that the residential program may be about to suggest that Charlie should return home. Not surprisingly, the longer they have enjoyed the peace of a Charlie-free house, the more they have worried about his return. Moreover, they wonder, "How can those child-care workers possibly have changed his behavior in such a short time?" They have no doubts about the competence of the residential staff. However, after all, most of them are young and do not have children of their own. The apparent success of the residential program reinforces the parents' sense of their own failure, and they seek reasons to put off the "dreaded day" of Charlie's return home. "Well, that's fine for them, but we could never give him the sort of full-time attention he has enjoyed there. He even seems to be enjoying himself. Of course he's doing better there—he gets lots of attention and doesn't have the day-to-day frustrations of home."

Finally, the residential counselor declares, "We have seen no tantrums from Charlie for some weeks now. I'm sure this problem is solved." They bring him home. It is good to have him back, but Charlie's parents are naturally cautious. They tend anxiously to be on the lookout for any hint of a return of problem behaviors and are thus less likely to notice those times he complies with a small direction or plays quietly with his sister. Rather, they cannot help but anticipate the day he begins to complain about a request or is even mildly uncooperative. "Ah, hah! We knew it wouldn't last."

The very "success" of the residential treatment leaves them with their failure as parents confirmed and contributes to a context within which they are much more likely to see "evidence" of continued pathology or of the transient nature of the success.

A Fictitious (but Typical) Residential Unit

Consider a residential unit—one which claims to use principles of systems-based family therapy. The structure is not unfamiliar. Children and adolescents are admitted because they, or their parents, or the state welfare department, or medical personnel, or the courts deem that they require treatment outside the home. Once each week, their families arrive for a family therapy session, wherein the "real" work is done. If the session goes well, the family might stay on for a meal with the child, or might take the child home for weekend leave. For the remainder of the time, the children and adolescents are cared for by child-care workers, who operate a program that includes a range of play and activity experiences, living-skills practice, and a high degree of control of difficult behavior.

The therapists believe that the therapy sessions are the main vehicle for bringing about change. They see the direct-care staff as doing little more than looking after the children in the time between therapy sessions. If a problem should arise, the job of the residential staff is to control the child until the next therapy session—or, if the problem is serious, until an extra session can be scheduled. The therapists do the "real" work.

The child-care workers, of course, often believe that the "real" work of change is done in *their* interactions with the children. Therapy is largely a self-indulgent activity carried out behind closed doors, which bears little relevance to the day-to-day program, which often disrupts the unit's schedule and upsets the children, and which results in additional instructions to be carried out in the coming week. It is okay for the therapists—they do not have to live with the children. They can construct elaborate interventions, but direct-care staff have to cope with the aftermath, which sometimes involves an increase in disturbed or disturbing behavior.

Of course, the therapists may harbor a conviction that residential treatment is a second-best option. If their therapy skills were better, they would be able to treat every family on an outpatient basis. Committed to notions of family therapy, they are never entirely happy with admitting the "identified patient" and involving the family only peripherally. They strive to develop their therapy skills, attending conferences and workshops, with the result that not only their clients but also their child-care colleagues are exposed to whatever is the latest intervention. The better their family therapy skills become, the less difference they seem to make in the day-to-day operation of the program, the greater the gulf becomes between what happens in the therapy room and what happens for the rest of the time on the residential unit. As this happens, the greater the tensions become between therapy and direct-care staff. Therefore, the more the direct-care staff tend to see their role as one of benevolent control.

Part of this pattern (for it is one that is repeated with alarming regularity) is the involvement and attitudes of the nonresidential family members. The program includes an extraordinarily high proportion of "resistant" families. Often, it is "discovered" that their commitment to their child is illusory. As the therapeutic program continues and the child or adolescent begins to show signs of greater control or stability, parents seem not always to share the optimism of the staff. They begin to find excuses for not having the child return home just yet, they accuse the unit of being too much like a "holiday camp," or they begin to "undermine" the therapeutic suggestions. Child-care staff may become protective of the children and develop negative opinions about the parents. There are longer staff meetings, as therapists help their direct-care colleagues work through their anger at being undermined or their feelings that certain parents are rejecting, unmotivated, or belligerent. When children finally return home, staff are dismayed at how quickly parents resume their previous complaints and how thoroughly they seem to reject the skills they have been taught.

DIFFERENT PROGRAMS — SIMILAR EXPERIENCES

Residential treatment is here to stay. However sophisticated our therapy skills become, however extensively we are able to establish community-based support services, I cannot imagine a time when there will not be court-ordered placements, or when there will not be children, adolescents, and parents who find it impossible to live together for the moment, or when there will not be families that require a period of distance for the

sake of safety or sanity. Services that seek to prevent residential placement, such as "intensive family based services" (Kinney, Haapala, & Booth,
1991), are an important addition to the mental health and welfare field;
however, their proponents are clear that these services do not mean that
placements never occur.

A degree of skepticism about residential placement is probably helpful.
Admitting a young person into a residential program too quickly is a sure
way to reinforce views of failure and/or pathology, and ignores the fact
that most families (with or without professional help) can find a way out
of their difficulties. Wanting "a break," or seeking someone else who will
"fix the problem," is an understandable and natural reaction to escalating
difficulties within the home. Nonetheless, most families can find the solution to their impasse if helped through the crisis. Having said this, I do
not believe that residential placement is inevitably a second-best solution.
The residential situation is one that can provide some space, and some
input, to allow families to begin the process of taking some control over
their lives. That it seems not to do so in many instances is not a reflection
on the inappropriateness of residential treatment as a form of intervention
but perhaps an indictment of our ideas about change, about families and
about people's strengths and resources in the residential arena—and the
way these are reflected in staffing policies and agency structure.

Brief family therapy, with its emphasis on interaction, on seeking to
avoid blame and labeling, and with its generally more positive focus, ought
to have much to offer the residential field. My experience suggests that
there are many residential programs that have embraced family therapy or
brief therapy in one of its manifestations. However, in many cases, family
therapy remains something done only in formal therapy sessions. The
remainder of the residential program appears largely untouched by so-
called systems ideas, and most of the units I know continue to base their
day-to-day operations on some kind of behavioral program, which seeks to
modify residents' behavior. This ranges from units that operate sophisticated regimes of reward and punishment, to those that embrace a less
rigorous climate of behavior control. Not only does this appear at odds
with the stated focus of the family therapy sessions, but it also perpetuates
a separation between the two aspects of the program.

In Australia, residential programs have evolved within a variety of contexts. Many residential units are part of nongovernment, nonprofit agencies (often with a church affiliation), many of which began life as orphan-
ages. Not surprisingly, the climate within which they developed was one
of "surrogate caring." Over the years, as the clientele has changed, the
mechanics of the units have altered but the philosophy remains substan-
tially the same. Some have evolved into small group homes, others into

homes using a "house-parent" model of care. The assumption underlying many has seemed to be "If we provide these disturbed children with enough, good enough, care, they will be able to overcome the damage done in their families and lead more successful lives." Staff tend to see their role as one of nurturing and somehow making up for the deficits that have existed in the children's care, and there has been little emphasis on seeing the program specifically as "therapeutic." It is not surprising that staff have often developed views of the children's parents as deficient or rejecting and that not only do parents appear reticent about their child's return home but staff also begin to worry about returning the child to that home environment.

The second arena within which residential programs have developed is that of the juvenile justice system — either in institutions operated by the state, often called "youth training centers," or in programs devised by other organizations as alternatives to correctional facilities. Over time, such programs have attempted to become more humane and have moved away from large-group institutions with custodial staff to smaller, more flexible units staffed by teams of youth workers or child-care workers. Given that most of the children and adolescents have brought with them a history of "acting out" or out-of-control behavior, the emphasis has usually been on control. The underlying assumption appears to be "If we can impose sufficient, consistent external control on these young people, they will be able to internalize that control and their behavior will change." The programs have been seen as seeking to modify behavior, with or without a specific focus on therapy. Staff often view their charges as conduct disordered or delinquent. Families are involved to varying degrees.

Some programs operate within the psychiatric hospital system (although this is more the case in the United States than in Australia). These programs show an inevitable focus on treatment and cure of some allegedly identifiable pathology, often driven by insurance companies' requirements for diagnosis. Such centers are usually more structured and entail a variety of group, individual, family, and milieu programs. However, despite their more "professional" appearance, the kind of children and adolescents who are the patients in these programs are not all that different from those who are in other programs. They are still young people who, for various reasons, are hard for their parents to deal with. Other programs operate as "youth refuges" and began life as places to which young people could go if they left their families and were effectively homeless. They are often staffed by youth workers, who may see their role as little more than providing a safe environment, and who are often more concerned with children's rights than family-based interventions.

The fact that some residential programs are located within the health system and others within the welfare system seems largely a result of historical or funding determinants. While there are differences among these programs, I am not certain that there are great differences in the types of children, adolescents, and parents they service. By and large, when a young person, for whatever reason, requires a period of out-of-home care or treatment, my experience is that the families feel defeated and demoralized, and the children or adolescents feel overwhelmed and as if their lives are slipping further and further away from their own control. To a greater or lesser extent, all these programs step in and assume some control over the family's situation. Families are often happy to "turn over" their child to the experts, yet this fact leaves them unable to feel much responsibility for any successful change.

A Context of Failure vs. a Context of Competence

What is of concern to me as I observe a variety of residential programs is *not* the specifics of what is done — specific interventions in therapy or specific activities in the more general program. Like most endeavors, there are good and bad residential programs and good and bad family therapy, and the particular theoretical or philosophical stance from which they come may not be the major determinant of this. What is of concern is the *context* within which these residential programs operate and which they, in turn, perpetuate.

According to the *Shorter Oxford Dictionary,* "context" is "the connection of the parts of a discourse" and "the parts which immediately precede or follow any particular passage or text and determine its meaning." That is, "context" has something to do with "connectedness" and with "meaning." According to Bateson (who inspired us to use the word in our original paper, but who acknowledges that it is a concept that is at least partly undefined — 1979, p. 15), "without context, words and action have no meaning at all."

In terms of common usage, it seems that we use the word "context" to refer to the milieu or general situation, which provides some clues or framework for interpreting actions. I have previously used the example of my talking with a group of psychiatric nurses, sitting in their staff room overlooking the grounds of the hospital. "You could do things and say things in here," I suggested, "that, if your patients did exactly the same things out there, you would immediately double their medication!" (Menses & Durrant, 1986). My suggestion was not simply an assertion that patients and nurses have different rights, but that the *context* represented and imposed by the hospital determined that actions on the part of patients would be interpreted as meaning one thing, and those same actions on the part of nurses as meaning another. Readers may be familiar with Rosenhan's famous research project, "On Being Sane in Insane Places" (Rosenhan, 1973), which showed how the context of the psychiatric hospital led to the "patients'" normal behavior being interpreted as part of their symptoms. That is, psychiatric diagnoses are "contextual" (Rosenhan, 1975). While allowing for individual differences, this tends to hold true as we move into different situations—or "contexts." The context determines how things are made sense of.

Later, Bateson wrote of a "changing of context—reframing" (Bateson & Bateson, 1987, p. 73). Reframing is a term with which most therapists are familiar and involves changing the meaning of a behavior by placing it in a different "frame" (Watzlawick, Weakland, & Fisch, 1974). Watzlawick, Weakland, and Fisch also speak of "a reality"—the particular way a situation is made sense of, which then determines how the participants will react to the situation.

Therefore, "context" may be seen as being similar to the terms "frame" (as in reframe), or "reality" (in Watzlawick's 1984 sense). I mean by "context" that matrix or framework of meanings that determines how people will make sense of a particular experience—what they think it is about.

In the situation of residential treatment, the *context* is the overall framework (or set of interlocking frameworks) that gives meaning to the placement and against which particular experiences and events will be interpreted. This context will be shaped by the structure of the program, the expectations clients, staff, and the wider society (public and professional) have of it, and the beliefs about themselves, each other, and their purpose that all parties bring to the encounter.

My concern about some residential programs is that many individually skillful and apparently successful activities and interventions occur but often within a context that mitigates against their ongoing success. That is, as long as residential placement occurs within a context built upon ideas of parental failure and/or child pathology, then even successful treatment will be made sense of in a way that will tend to reinforce those preexisting beliefs. The context of placement involves the way the child or adolescent and the other family members make sense of themselves in this situation ("We have failed"; "He/she is disturbed"; "I am bad"; etc.) *and* the way residential staff make sense of themselves and their roles. These beliefs or constructs provide the template against which apparent success or failure will be interpreted.

Given that residential placement is often a "last resort," families have usually been well-schooled in notions of their own failure, incompetence, or pathology. Having been caught on a slide (or a rollercoaster, with its ups and downs) of attempts to deal with their situation, seeking help, perhaps feeling hopeful and then having these hopes dashed, it is not surprising that families approach a residential placement as being yet more of the same. In desperation, they will try anything, although they may suspect that this, too, will not really work. When the agency does what they (or someone else) asks, and admits their child, this is confirmation of all they have believed about themselves and/or their child. The context is inevitably one of incompetence, and what is surprising is that residential treatment sometimes works, given that we might expect ideas of incompetence to permeate everything that happens.

The problem, of course, with the beliefs and ideas that contribute to the residential context — the residential "reality," if you like — is that the participants believe them. They gain the status of reality. The more I, as a parent, "know" that I am a failure, the more I will see evidence that confirms this, the more I will interpret the helpful suggestions of residential staff as revealing that they consider me a failure, and so on. I will have no conceptual means for interpreting things in any other way. Similarly, the more I, as a residential worker, "know" that particular parents are unmotivated, the more I will see evidence that confirms this and the more I will respond to them in an adversarial manner.

In reconsidering residential treatment, then, our task is not primarily one of tinkering with the mechanics of residential programs. In fact, we can tinker all we like but, as long as the context or meaning-frame for family and staff remains the same, we are doing little more than window-dressing. What we need to reconsider is the overall context. How do we make sense of the phenomenon of residential placement? How do our clients make sense of it? Is there a way of "reframing" — not just reframing this particular presenting problem, but placing the whole experience of residential treatment within a different frame — one that will maximize the possibility of clients experiencing themselves as competent and successful? Of course, any such change in the way we *think* about residential placement will have implications for the day-to-day details of any program and for the interrelations between the different people involved (who is the expert at what?), and the day-to-day details will contribute to the extent to which any frame persists. However, my major concern is with formulating ways of thinking about residential admissions which may provide a coherent template for considering every aspect of the program.

NEW MEANING MAKES NEW BEHAVIOR POSSIBLE

My concern is with the way we think about what we do — and the way our clients think about what they do and what we do. What continues to surprise me about my own original profession is that people seem to believe that psychologists *know* something. Moreover, some psychologists seem to believe it, too! Yet, if behavior is influenced by context, the meaning of behavior is not fixed, and people are not as predictable as our systems of classification might suggest. A focus on context is a focus on meaning, and meaning is not a fixed entity. I do not believe that therapy or residential treatment should be about identifying some recognizable problem and modifying people's behavior or dealing with the underlying causes. I believe therapy should be about establishing conditions in which people can make sense of themselves differently, and thus respond differently.

My underlying assumption is that we are all engaged in a constant process of making sense of our experience. In elaborating this point, we might refer to Kelly's (1955, 1963) idea about "personal constructs," which determine how we all make sense of our experience, or we might use Bateson's (1979) idea of "restraints," which are beliefs that prevent our seeing things in different ways, or ideas of self-concept. All these concepts are concerned with the way in which individuals and groups make sense of themselves within their experience of life's events. Meaning is not immutable, and our behavior and emotion will be determined by how we make sense of our situation, our relationships, and our experiences.

Problems reflect people being stuck* in a particular way of making sense of things, and this way of seeing means that alternative behaviors or possibilities for solution are not available to them. Watzlawick, Weakland, and Fisch suggest that problems often happen because normal life events and experiences are made sense of in a particular way that leads them to attempt to solve the problem in a particular way. Even if these attempts do not seem to work, they tend to resort to "more of the same" solutions, since their explanation of the situation does not allow room for alternative solutions (Watzlawick et al., 1974; Weakland et al., 1974). This concept of more of the same attempted solutions leading inexorably to more of the same problem is a central idea in the brief approaches to therapy.

Cade has summarized this assumption

> As our patterns of association become established in a particular way, they will tend to influence the processing of subsequent experiences. . . . In this way we develop belief frameworks or mental "sets" that determine how we see ourselves and our world, and how we ascribe meaning, and thus respond to, those experiences. In our relationships with others, we

*In reference to the phenomenon of "more of the same," I have commented that, if I was ever to be asked to contribute to a revision of *DSM*, my version would include only one diagnostic category — that of "stuck" — which would encompass all the existing diagnostic categories (Durrant & Kowalski, 1993).

then develop patterns of behaving together that both reflect our mental sets and those of the people with whom we interact, and tend by repetition to be confirmed—though such patterns rarely develop consciously. (Cade, 1985, p. 35)

I believe that, in our work with children and families, we cannot know why things happen (and, often, our clients themselves do not know). We can make guesses (or "hypotheses"), which may be more or less helpful. Our focus, then, becomes one not of our knowing why things happen but of how our clients make sense of their experience and how we might assist them to make sense of things differently. A focus on context leads us to operate our residential programs in such a way as to make it most likely that people will experience new possibilities, that they will find ways of seeing themselves that will provide new options for relationships and behavior.

2

RITES of PASSAGE:

PRACTICING BEING

DIFFERENT

How Do We Think About What We Do?

We have two ways of thinking about the task of residential treatment (or any therapy, for that matter). We can consider it a process in which we therapists act upon the child and/or family in order to change them or to repair damage, or we can consider it a process in which we work with children and families to assist them in changing themselves. No matter how we dress up what we do, I believe that all therapeutic encounters reflect one or the other of these underlying ideas. Further, the way we think about what it is we do will determine most of what happens and will strongly influence how our clients respond and view themselves during and after the process.

Much residential work has reflected ideas of children being damaged or disturbed, children possessing some problem or pathology, or parents being incompetent or deficient. If we approach our task from this viewpoint, inevitably we will see our role as that of experts who operate upon the clients in order to fix or cure something. This view may be reflected in providing therapeutic care to help children "get over" damaging experiences, exerting control to modify unacceptable behavior and allow control to be internalized, prescribing tasks to alter dysfunctional family structure or processes, and so on. As I have suggested in the previous chapter, however well such interventions may be achieved they inevitably reinforce a context of family incompetence. Clients may enter treatment ex-

12

periencing themselves as having the *status* of failures or people who are deficient. They may leave treatment with the immediate problem solved but with their status confirmed, since they may not have experienced themselves as having much personal agency or control over the process of change.

When my European car (a Peugeot) breaks down, I seek an expert to repair it. I have taken some time to search out a mechanic who understands the intricacies of French automobiles, and "George" is a wonderful expert who can fix any problem that my car develops. I have no delusions about having any ability myself to repair my car, and I marvel at George's abilities to diagnose and repair (and, if I ever begin to think that I can repair my car, George tells me, "Michael, you stick to people and I'll stick to cars!"). Whenever he returns the car to me with the problem solved, this reinforces my view that I am incompetent in matters of European mechanics (and the size of his bill reminds me of his expertise!). Fortunately, my view of my own expertise regarding cars is not a major contributor to my overall self-concept. Nonetheless, I leave his garage pleased that the car now functions but confirmed in my view of my own lack of expertise in this area. The problem is solved; however, the broader context — which contributes to my view of my own status in the matter — has been strengthened. Sadly, children are often taken to residential programs in much the same way that cars are taken to workshops. The family, understandably, wants them to be repaired; however, the successful repair may confirm their lack of expertise. Society does not expect me to have skills in repairing cars. However, society *does* expect competence in parents, hence the implications of this lack of expertise are more serious.

In my approach to therapy and residential treatment, I have found assumptions about deficit and repair unhelpful. They sit poorly alongside my view, and my observations, that people and families are resourceful entities, which manage to cope well with a multitude of pressures, changes, and difficulties. Of course, when they come to me, clients may be coping or functioning less effectively, but this does not change the fact that most of the time most people manage most pressures in ways that work for them. One of the problems with being a therapist (or a residential worker) is that our views are derived from inadequate or "skewed" data. We see clients when things are *not* going well, and such a skewed sample easily leads us to see the world in terms of dysfunction, pathology, and deficit.

Of course, our forebears in the realm of individually-oriented therapy and psychiatry reflected this focus most clearly in that operation known as diagnosis. Once a problem has been classified in a so-called objective manner, it ceases to exist in the *experience* of clients but now exists within a body of expert knowledge about what is normal and healthy and what is abnormal and unhealthy. It matters little whether the specific formulation is rendered in terms of analytic theory, bonding and attachment theory, learning theory, systems theory, ideas about entities such as "A.D.D.," or any other theory. Once we have identified the type of problem, and perhaps its underlying causes, we have entered the realm of deficit and repair, and we confine ourselves to a position that obscures from our view any strengths or successes that might otherwise be evident or possible in the lives of our clients.

Family therapy has not been immune from this. Despite a stated emphasis on systems and "circular causality," family therapists have resorted to identifying family pathology, dysfunctional family structures, conflictual marriages as "causing" children's problems, and so on. While our classificatory systems may not have been as microscopically sophisticated, the result of the way in which we describe and make sense of what our clients present, and therefore of what is our role, has often been remarkably similar to that of therapeutic models many family therapists have otherwise claimed to reject.

However, within the brief and family therapy arenas, there have been challenges to this prevailing orthodoxy. The original (and continuing) approach to brief therapy of the MRI group in Palo Alto (Watzlawick et al., 1974; Weakland et al., 1974) has been "non-normative and non-pathological" (Heath & Ayers, 1991), and others have built their frameworks and approaches on assumptions about clients' strengths rather than clients' deficiencies. Often referring to Milton Erickson's focus on *utilizing* what clients bring to therapy rather than simply imposing preconceived therapist ideas about what should happen, many therapists have embraced approaches that seek to *work with* rather than *operate upon* clients—and it is only possible to work *with* if we have a fundamental assumption that people can achieve solutions to their difficulties. The "solution-focused brief therapy" approach of de Shazer and his colleagues (de Shazer, 1988, 1991) rests on the assumption that there are times clients are doing things right, and that it is more useful to focus on these than on what they are doing "wrong." O'Hanlon (1993) talks of "possibility therapy," grounded in the firm belief that change is a possibility and that clients simply have to realize this. Papp (1988) refers to such approaches as representing a *resource model*, " . . . in which the therapist views families as essentially resourceful and only secondarily and temporarily in need of therapy. In the resource model the therapist searches for and uses the family's own strengths and resources rather than viewing the family as deficient and needing repair from outside sources" (p. v).

Instead of concentrating our efforts on identifying and correcting pathology, we should concentrate on shoring up and amplifying people's resources and strengths. People are more likely to cooperate and change
in an environment that supports their strength and resourcefulness, and
that offers a view of them as capable, than they are when focused on
pathology and problems. (O'Hanlon, 1990, p. 88)

Residential programs are particularly vulnerable to notions of deficit
and repair. After all, that is often what parents want or expect — "Take my
child and fix whatever it is that is wrong." That is often what courts and
social welfare agencies expect. Moreover, the very fact of taking a child or
adolescent *out* of the home and family environment and placing him or
her *into* a special program reinforces the view that something special is
happening here. In the nonresidential setting, it is easier for us to claim a
nonpathological stance. The act of residential admission seems to confirm
that this is the person who is or has the problem and we are the experts
who will operate a program to cure it. However, my recurring theme is
that such a view contributes to a context that leaves child and family with
the same status of incompetence as they had before.

If we truly believe that the children, adolescents, and families we see
are capable of experiencing competence in their lives (for a *belief* is what
it is), then this presents particular challenges for the residential situation.
How can we construct a context, for ourselves as well as for our clients,
that will contribute to the experience of competence? We may employ
the methods of brief, solution-focused, or resource therapy, but these are
insufficient in themselves unless they happen within a more general climate that allows the entire residential program to reflect their values.
Somehow attaching a resource-based approach to therapy onto a more
generally and implicitly deficit-based residential program is a recipe for
confusion and staff conflict. Rather, the question is "Is there a way in
which we can *think* about the entire residential process that will further
our aims of enhancing competence and harnessing resources?"

This focus on competence has been influencing aspects of mental
health and welfare work in a variety of settings. As mentioned in the
previous chapter, there are a number of approaches to therapy that have
emerged and that are founded on ideas about competence (de Shazer,
1988, 1991; O'Hanlon & Weiner-Davis, 1989; for example). Further, the
"intensive family-based services" and "placement prevention" approaches,
particularly the "Homebuilders'" model (Kinney, Haapala, & Booth, 1991),
assume that families have strengths and the ability to change. Given that
these approaches are not always successful in preventing placement, it is

helpful if an ensuing placement happens in a way that reflects similar ideas about competence.

CHANGE—CURING A PROBLEM OR TRANSITION BETWEEN STATUSES?

What do we think change is? If we begin from a premise that our clients have resources and that they have handled lots of challenges successfully, we may understand the predicament with which they present as one in which they are "stuck." They have tried to do something about the situation but this has not worked, and they have become caught in seeing themselves as incompetent or failures. That is, the context is one of failure, their status one of incompetence. We might suggest that a process of change will aim at allowing them to experience themselves differently—to see themselves within a different context or as having a different status. Therefore, our aim is not to cure. Our aim is to assist a transition between one status and another—that is, status as perceived by themselves and by those with whom they have been involved in the community around their particular difficulty. Treatment as a process of transition holds quite different implications from treatment as a process of cure or modification.

The anthropological literature offers ways of thinking about the process of change as a transition between different statuses, and it is here that we find a metaphor for the process of residential treatment, which might facilitate a climate of developing or recognizing competence. Given that there is much about the process of residential treatment that is divorced from the normal processes of everyday life, it may be helpful to consider the literature about *ritual* processes, or processes that symbolize the process of change. In particular, van Gennep (1908) has written of that class of ritual processes that he terms "rites of passage," which are ritual processes that involve a transition between life stages or statuses.

We might think of a family approaching the residential treatment of their child as being within a context of failure and seeing themselves as having the status of failures. Our hope is that they will emerge from the process within a context of competence, experiencing themselves as having the status of success. The metaphor of a "rite of passage" (for we must remember that *any* explanatory or theoretical concept we apply to what we do is only a metaphor—our clients do not necessarily experience it in the same way that we describe it) appears relevant to a process that involves a change in status or context.

In many tribal cultures, much is made of the transition from boyhood to manhood, or girlhood to womanhood, and a complex ritual process often surrounds this transition. For example, at the appointed time, the boys leave the tribe (and, in a sense, leave behind their boyhood) and go out into the wilderness. There, they practice hunting, fighting, stalking prey, and so on — in essence, they practice or experiment with being adult. During this time, they are neither child nor adult — they are in transition. After a suitable period of practice, they rejoin the tribe and are hailed as adults. In many ways, this may appear premature. Clearly they have not experienced everything there is to being adult, and their learning and development will continue. Physically, they are only a few weeks older than before and so are not identifiably adult, in terms of being physically different. Nonetheless, they return as adults and are regarded in terms of their new status from that point onward. Usually, there is then some celebration, which entails a public acknowledgment of their new status.

When thinking of rituals in general, and rites of passage in particular, it is easy to think of the celebration as being the rite of passage. As van Gennep (1908) has shown, the celebration is only the endpoint of the rite of passage. The essence of the process is in the transition between two statuses, and the period of transition or practice is what marks this process. The entire ritual process provides a framework within which the transition may take place. A ritual, such as a rite of passage, "can therefore not just *mark* a transition, but also *make* a transition at the same time" (Roberts, 1988, p. 14).

If we consider residential treatment as a means by which a family is helped to negotiate a transition between two statuses or directions, the rite of passage metaphor may allow us to shape the program in such a way as to facilitate this. However thorough a program may be, any family will face continued challenges after their child or adolescent has been discharged. Rather than seeing our goal as one of cure, I prefer to see us as helping families start out on a different path, with new skills and new feelings of competence. We may consider the program (and its ultimate completion) as *marking* a transition for a child and family, but also that the program itself helps them *make* this transition. Others have suggested the rite of passage metaphor as an analogy for the process of therapy itself (Imber-Black, Roberts, & Whiting, 1988; Kobak & Waters, 1984). The metaphor seems to fit the residential treatment situation even better.

RESIDENTIAL TREATMENT AS A RITE OF PASSAGE

Van Gennep (1908) describes the rite of passage as a ritual process with three stages.

In the first stage, *separation*, special preparations are made and new knowledge is passed on as the frame is set for marking a particular event.

The time of preparing for the ritual is as important a part of the ritual process as the actual event itself. The second stage is the *liminal or transitional,* where people actually partake of the ritual and experience themselves in new ways and take on new roles, new identities. The third stage is *reaggregation or reintegration* where people are reconnected to their community with their new status. (Roberts, 1988, p. 7–8)

We may consider these three stages as they apply to the residential situation, for they may provide a useful framework in which to construct our view of the residential process.

Separation Stage

When a child or adolescent is admitted to a residential program there is an obvious separation—a separation within the family. However, that is not the separation that we wish to highlight, for that separation easily reinforces views of the child's fault or deficit. If we are to encourage this as a time of transition for the whole family, we do not want the physical separation of child from parents to be the major focus (and, as will be seen, the task of finding creative and consistent ways to involve the non-residential family members in the treatment is a crucial one). Rather, the process of admission may be seen as one in which the child and family together begin to separate from their problem and their past.

"Rites of passage begin when persons separate from an old status that no longer fits for them." (Adams-Westcott & Isenbart, 1990, p. 38). That is, the separation we need to highlight is a separation at the level of context or status—not the separation of people from one another.

We do not want the residential treatment to be "more of the same." They have probably had previous attempts at therapy and, if they are now seeking a residential placement (which is often seen as the "end of the line"), these may have been unsuccessful, demoralizing and probably have lessened hope that things might improve. It is easy for the residential admission to fit into this pattern and to become another step on the same well-trodden path towards incompetence rather than a first step on a new path of hopefulness and competence. Separation, then, is separation from former ways of seeing the situation and it involves a number of aspects.

First, it is important that parents and child experience validation of their experience and their efforts. For those who work in residential programs, it is easy to become blasé about a new admission and to forget what a huge step it is for parents and child alike. If we wish to make this a period of transition rather than an act of cure, we will want our clients to experience themselves as having a major role to play in what happens. We will want to work *with* them rather than *on* them. To achieve this relationship, we will need to begin from a stance that displays genuine respect and validation—and adopting this stance will sorely test what we have learned to believe about our clients. We do not wish to downplay the step of presenting for admission. It is important that our clients experience us as appreciative of the efforts they have made and as understanding their doubts and fears and frustrations. Further, they need to hear us acknowledging that they have made an important decision in seeking this placement. Of course, their experience may be that they had no choice—either because the situation seemed intolerable or because an external agent has made the decision about the placement—nonetheless, it is helpful to begin from the view that the residential admission represents a choice on the part of parents and child, a choice to work on change.

Second, the separation stage involves building a different way to view the placement that will allow it to become a transition. This is a process of *reframing*—not just reframing the presenting problem as we might do in therapy, but reframing the whole process of treatment. This reframing may employ externalizing the problem for child and family (White, 1989), it may involve framing the situation in terms of building on success rather than overcoming failure; however, it will certainly include framing the placement as a period of practice or experimentation. This process of reframing is an essential part of the preparation for the admission and the creation of a context of transition, and is described in detail in the following chapter. This process seeks to establish a way of thinking about the placement that will highlight the family's strengths and make it most likely that they will cooperate in embarking on a new direction.

"Rituals are co-evolved symbolic acts that include not only the ceremonial aspects of the actual presentation of the ritual, but the process of preparing for it as well. It . . . [has] both open and closed parts which are 'held' together by a guiding metaphor." (Roberts, 1988, p. 8). What Roberts means by "open" and "closed" parts of the ritual are those parts of the process that will allow flexibility and are not structured and those parts of the process that are predetermined or part of the structure. What is important here is her suggestion that the various parts of the process are "held together" by a guiding metaphor. Reframing the residential placement will provide a metaphor for the task that becomes a *theme* for child, family, and residential staff as the various aspects of the program proceed. This theme will set the current process apart from previous attempts at solution and will provide a shared language and way of thinking that may be used throughout all that follows. The theme that flows from the reframing may be graphic, such as "intensive itch-fighting practice" for a girl who had "itchy fingers" and stole money (Menses & Durrant, 1986), or more general, such as "an opportunity to practice overcoming the pattern you have got stuck in" for a young man and his father (Durrant & Coles, 1991), or "practicing having more good days" (as in the example in Chapter 4); however, it will provide some coherence to the placement. The theme establishes a way of thinking about the new direction on which the family is embarking, and the family's future life with the child must be a part of this stage as well as at the time of discharge.

An important aspect of the creation of the theme is that it suggests a meaning for the situation that is different to that held by all participants previously. Previous meanings most likely included the idea of the child or adolescent being at fault or disturbed and/or of the parents being deficient, and such meanings are not conducive to ideas of child, family, and staff working cooperatively. The new theme places the coming experience in a different frame, in which all participants are facing challenges together. The practical situation may be that the child is moving into the residential unit, however, the meaning given to the process encompasses everyone. "These moves have the important function of treating all family members as common travellers *who are equal in their need and hope for change*" (Kobak & Waters, 1984, p. 91). The process of transition will be a process that the whole family will be undergoing, not just the child.

LIMINAL OR TRANSITION STAGE

I have told a number of families, when negotiating the admission of their son or daughter, that I cannot guarantee that the problem will be solved by the time their child returns home. Moreover, I have said, home is the only place where change can occur. They do not live in the residential unit, so any changes or achievements made there will be important lessons and may provide ideas about how to do things differently at home, but will not in themselves change the situation at home.

If we see placement as transition rather than cure, the pressure is off us to solve this problem during a delineated time period. The removal of that pressure means that we do not have to be looking constantly for evidence of steady improvement. Rather, we can see the time as one of ups and downs, one of experimenting with or practicing new ways of doing things. Change of any sort, and particularly change in the way family members interact and see themselves, will not be immediate and may not be steady. Whenever we make a change in what we do, accompanied by a change in how we think of ourselves, we go through a period of trial and error. This is the natural human experience. Most of us did not know immediately how to be a spouse. We may have had a period of engagement in which to "try out" being part of a couple and, for most people, that period of engagement included misunderstandings, times of despondency, and times of excitement as we experimented with this relationship. Similarly, when I left the hospital setting and ventured into private practice as a therapist, my first few months were marked by experimenting with systems, organizing and reorganizing the way I did things, trying out my new freedom and recognizing my new responsibilities. For some time it felt as if I was "playing" at private practice, since there was a period of trial and error before I was able to feel comfortable with my new identity. If this is our experience as we negotiate "normal" life-cycle changes, how much more will it be the case when people embark on changing themselves in relation to a situation they have experienced as painfully problematic?

Bateson (1979) spoke of change and learning as a "stochastic process," by which he meant a process of random or new experiences that are experienced by trial and error. In tribal initiation rites, the initiates practice or experiment with being adult. There is not an expectation that, as soon as they have left childhood behind, they will automatically know how to be adult. Moreover, what they achieve through this process of liminality is the status of seeing themselves as adult, not a final level of skill in all adult activities. The trial-and-error process is one of trying out new ways of thinking about themselves, since these will provide the framework for them to go on in their new role. "In the marginal or liminal stage, the person or group going through the ritual is in neither old status nor the new one. . . . [they] try out new roles, new identities" (Roberts, 1988, p. 19).

The period of the residential placement may be seen as one part of the transitional stage, in which everything is viewed as experimental or practice or "trial and error." The advantage of the residential situation for the child or adolescent is that it may provide a venue for intensive practice and a safe context for experimentation. The advantage of the residential placement for the parents is that it may provide some physical distance that will allow them to practice or experiment without the immediate pressure of their child being at home. This concept of practice or experimenting is stressed throughout the placement. People have been stuck in patterns of behaving and relating that have not worked for them, and they may take some time to figure out new ways that will work. Such a way of thinking is in sharp contrast to many expectations that the child in placement will improve in a regular, step-wise fashion. That expectation, whether explicit or implicit, leaves little room for slip-ups to be seen as anything other than failures. Yet we ought to expect that old familiar behaviors and patterns will persist and that even acknowledged progress will be marked by periods that are less successful.

I have seen too many children and parents whose excitement about progress is shattered by a single incident that is seen as failure or regression. Yet, if we think about practice — practicing hitting a ball, practicing a part in a play, practicing a musical instrument, and so on — we would learn little if we always got it right. It is the times we make mistakes that help us be clearer about the way we want things to be and about what not to do next time. I have also seen too many instances of a child or adolescent being admitted to a residential program with a particular problem, and then summarily discharged for displaying that problem. (The most striking example is when a young person is admitted to the program because he or she is violent, and then discharged because he or she is violent. That is not to say that we must tolerate unbridled violence. However, I cannot help but feel that this may easily become yet another experience of failure and make the prospect of change seem even more remote.)

All behavior within the program is seen as experimental. This does not mean that there is no behavior that may *not* be acceptable and may attract consequences (and I discuss the way in which we might think about "discipline" and "consequences" in Chapter 8). Nonetheless, the climate of the program is one in which everything is seen in terms of practice. These young people, and their families, are in a stage of "betwixt and between." They are in a period of transition. If they could achieve success immediately and consistently, they would not be in the program! A climate or framework of practice is not licence to do anything, not a prescription for staff to tolerate anything. Rather, it offers a way of thinking about the process, which should (coupled with the theme developed before admission) give us ways to respond to behavior and discuss events that further the move towards competence and control.

In practical terms, the task of residential staff during this stage is one of highlighting "exceptions" to previous behavior (de Shazer et al., 1986) and talking about these as experimental discoveries on which progress can be built, as well as discussing "setbacks" as part of the ongoing experimentation. There may or may not be a specific, more structured aspect to the program for a particular resident; however, this, along with day-to-day experiences, provides the material for discussion in terms of practice. Just as I have suggested that it is the way we *think* about residential treatment that is important, so it is the way we talk about what happens and respond to behaviors and events that is more important than the events themselves. As far as the nonresidential family members are concerned, concurrent therapy sessions and other ways of their being involved in the program similarly seek continually to define their "work" at home as an integral and **equally** important part of the experimental task.

Our overriding aim is that families who have experienced failure and lack of control will discover that they can be successful and can exercise control in their lives. In keeping with this, everything that happens during the transitional stage is discussed with them. If a specific program is involved, or particular behavior on the part of their child is causing difficulties, their assistance is sought. No decisions are made about the resident's program separate from consultation with his or her family. This stance may be very different from that common in some residential programs, where staff are the experts who make treatment decisions about clients. However, if any gains made during the placement are to persist after discharge, parents will need to see themselves as competent and effective. They are more likely to feel able to continue with any changes if they have experienced themselves as part of the process of achieving those changes. After all, as we might say to parents, we may have some expertise in creating an environment that facilitates experimentation and change, but they know their own child and family situation far better than we do, and they are more knowledgeable about what will or will not be helpful. In addition, we might continually highlight the fact that the residential setting is an artificial context. It will possibly be tougher "out there."

Reincorporation or Completion Stage

In one sense, practice never ends. I continue to practice and experiment with being a private practitioner and, hopefully, I will keep on learning. I continue to experiment with being a spouse, and often I make mistakes from which (one hopes) I learn. The adult initiates have before them years of continued practice at being adult, and they have not mastered every skill by the end of the ritual initiation. The end of the ritual process does not mean that the change has finished. Nonetheless, in the same way that I now see myself as a private practitioner and view myself as a husband and father, the young people in the tribe have achieved the status of adult, however falteringly may be their expression of this.

If the residential placement continues until new behaviors are consolidated and setbacks never occur, it will never end. The completion of the process is *not* when child and family have surmounted every problem or challenge, but when they have had sufficient practice to help them feel confident about taking on the challenges back at home. That is, it is when they have begun to see themselves as competent and ready to embark upon their new direction as a family. If we see residential treatment as cure, we will find ourselves trying to convince parents that their son or daughter is ready to return home, we will find them raising obstacles to this return, and we may expect them to be on the lookout for any sign that things have not worked. If we see residential treatment as a period of transition, then the ritual process will be complete before every aspect of the situation is resolved.

The stage of completion or reincorporation is one in which child and family are ready to commence the *real* work together. Parents and child will have been involved in monitoring each other's progress in experimenting and will have learned from themselves and each other. The future will still appear tentative; however, the possibility of a different future will be a real possibility. Kobak and Waters suggest that the task of the therapist (or residential staff, I would suggest) during the transitional period of treatment "is to maintain the family *on the threshold of possibilities*" (1984, p. 94). Having been stuck in seeing their situation as hopeless and having felt powerless to achieve anything themselves, the end of a period of experimentation should be one in which child and family see the possibility of things being different and have experienced the possibility of seeing themselves as competent.

As we seek to "reincorporate" the family into its ongoing life (for the ritual process of residential treatment has been a period divorced, in some ways, from the realities of everyday life), we will use conceptualizations of a different future to help them build their own agenda for continuing with change. The theme or therapeutic frame will gradually recede—it was part of the ritual process and everyone knew it was merely symbolic. The focus will shift to the realities and pragmatics of what new ideas and learnings, new views of self, will mean for home and school and work. Therapy sessions, both at the time of discharge and in the period of follow-up, will revolve around those things that were practiced and seen to work, and how they might be continued in the ongoing process of doing the *real* work of change.

A Celebration

The entire process of residential treatment may be seen as a ritual process, using the metaphor of a rite of passage. Nonetheless, more specific ritual events will be an important part of the process. The completion of practice or experimenting warrants a celebration, and such a celebration deserves all the seriousness (and serious enjoyment) of a ritual celebration. The celebration is the public proclamation of a new status. It is the sign to everyone that the person is no longer to be thought of as before. The celebration of adulthood is a sign that, henceforth, these young people will be regarded as adult. Others may realize their youth and lack of skill, nonetheless, they will be regarded as adult and their ongoing practice will be viewed in those terms. My own graduation was a public declaration that I was now to be afforded the status of graduate psychologist. Previously, I had the status of student, and both my successes and failures were made sense of within the confines of that status. After graduation, my successes and failures were to be understood within a different context. There was not an expectation that suddenly I would be successful in every professional endeavor; however, no matter how much I might make mistakes, I could never return to my former status. I now thought of myself differently, as did others.

The discharge party or celebration is not just a chance for expressing relief and being happy about success. It is an important marker of a change of status, and is both happy and solemn. Things will never quite be the same again, for both family and community now see things differently. Some of the old behaviors will persist — it would be surprising if they did not — however, they may now be seen as an ongoing challenge rather than more evidence of failure.

After the Transition . . . the *Real* Work

Australia prides itself on its prowess in aquatic sports. One of the major national preoccupations, every four years as the Olympic Games approach, is whether our swimming team will be able to surpass the teams from the United States and Eastern Europe. Being an island continent, water is important to us, and we feel that swimming is one sport at which we should excel. We have our share of gold medals, yet we remain in the shadow of other swimming teams. I can only imagine that our swimmers see themselves in terms of continued failure (and certainly, while the entire country hails any gold medal winner, we take little comfort in our athletes coming second).

Before every major competition, such as the Olympic contest, our swimmers go "on retreat." That is, they have a residential placement. They go away together for a period of intensive training. Away from the pressures of day-to-day life — the phone calls, the media, the gaze of would-be critics and swimming experts — they live in a practice environment where they may experiment with new strategies, develop their skills, and begin to see themselves as winners. The advantages of getting away to achieve this are obvious. Nonetheless, this time is only one of practice. They cannot actually win medals during this time. No matter how fast they swim, times achieved during practice do not constitute world records. Nothing that happens or is achieved changes the fact that they have to venture to the Games themselves and face the real competition.

If residential treatment is a period of transition, an opportunity for practice, it does not change the fact that the real work is still to be done. After the celebration, when the young person returns home, the task is not finished — it is only beginning. The task of reorganizing family relationships and implementing new behaviors is ahead. It is only back in the home environment that ongoing change can really be achieved. Our hope is that, by the end of the residential placement, family members have discovered and experienced new possibilities and now see themselves as ready and equipped to take on new challenges together. Our hope is that they have experienced themselves as having a different status, which will allow them to face the uncertainty and trepidation of change from a different standpoint.

Residential treatment does not solve problems.

What it does is offer an opportunity for families to make the transition from feeling hopeless and helpless to feeling that they have some skills and ideas about how to go forward.

David, aged 12, had longstanding difficulties with his temper. His parents had felt overwhelmed by this and had doubted their own abilities. After previously unsuccessful therapy, David entered the residential unit for intensive practice in fighting the Temper. It was clear that the Temper had interfered with David's growing up, and his time in the residential program was a chance to practice getting on with his own growing up.

In his time in the program, David had a chance to experiment with responding to frustration in different ways, and staff ensured that David experienced situations of frustration from time to time. At the same time, his parents used the time that David was in the residential unit to practice consolidating their view of themselves as a parental unit and to try out, with their other children and with David when he returned on weekend leave, different ways of responding to Tempers. They experimented with not allowing the Temper to upset them or distract them from their view of themselves as parents who knew best, and they practiced ignoring the Temper and insisting on their rules despite the Temper's efforts to deflect them. Both David and his parents discovered that there were many times already that they were getting on together without allowing the Temper to intervene. Taming the Temper became the theme for the placement, and staff responded to David both in terms of specific examples of his not letting the Temper gain control and also in terms of more general evidence of his being someone who showed signs of strength and control.

During his time in the program, youth workers discovered that David had a particular interest in boxing. They began to talk with him in terms of the times the Temper "had him on the ropes" and the times he had the Temper "down for the count." In his discharge celebration, in which David and his parents joined with staff to celebrate the fact that they had completed intensive training in Temper fighting, David was presented with a "Champion Temper Tamer" certificate. His parents seemed pleased to receive "Champion Temper Taming Coaches" certificates. David was given a boxing trophy—a bronze figure on a wooden pedestal, with three plaques on the base. The first of these had been engraved to signify that David was a Champion Temper Tamer; however, it was made clear that this plaque referred only to Round One. The remaining plaques were for Rounds Two and Three, and David and his family were left to decide when these should be engraved. On the one hand, they had each had their new status confirmed. On the other hand, it was clear that the majority of the task lay before them and that they would be the judges of continued success.

— Timaru Hostel, Care Force Youth Services, Sydney

SUMMARY — SO WHAT'S IT ALL ABOUT?

This and the preceding chapter have outlined the theoretical concepts that provide a way of thinking about residential programs. The remainder of the book will consider various aspects of the residential program and offer some ideas about how the concepts might make a difference to clients, families, and residential staff.

The way we *think* about what we do has profound implications for every aspect of the residential program. The way we think about residential treatment will not only affect any more formal therapy activities but will also affect how we handle matters of discipline within the residential unit, how we respond to different behaviors, what we say to parents, and so on.

Here, then, is a very brief summary of the major concepts or principles that lie behind the methods outlined in the rest of the book.

1. People are engaged in a constant process of "making sense of" themselves, their relationships, and what happens to them. This view of self (or constructs) is what determines how people feel and behave. Therefore, a residential program must take into consideration how young people and their families make sense of the treatment — that is, a focus on the meaning of everything that happens.

2. When people in families have problems it is a reflection of their getting "stuck." Their view of self means that they often do not see the possibility of things being different and so may feel hopeless and defeated, and may get caught up in continuing problem behavior.

3. People have resources and strengths and are capable of behaving differently, but their way of thinking about themselves and their behavior often means that they do not see these strengths. The

views that residential staff have about their clients, and about their own role, often means that they do not see the clients' strengths either.

4. A residential program based on ideas of modifying problem behavior or curing psychological or emotional problems will easily promote a context that leaves residents and families feeling more incompetent or disempowered, even if the treatment is apparently successful, and may work against any changes continuing once the family is reunited.

5. Residential placement may be "framed" as a transition from one way of viewing self to another—from a status of failure and problem to one of success and solution. As a time of transition, it will be marked by practice and experimenting—with inevitable "ups and downs" rather than an expectation of constant progress.

6. Everything that happens as part of the treatment will either promote or work against this transition. The way the placement is framed can provide a "theme" that gives some consistency to every aspect of the program and provides a framework for planning and responding during the admission.

7. Our aim is to work *with* children, adolescents and families, rather than to work *on* them.

> The aim of residential treatment is that the young person and his or her family should be able to experience themselves as competent and successful. It is through this process that they may develop a new view of self, which will allow for the ongoing discovery of more helpful, acceptable, and successful behavior.

3

ESTABLISHING a
THEME for PRACTICE

Not all residential programs work from a clearly articulated theory of change or include a formal therapy component, yet most programs I know aim to be therapeutic. In fact, I suspect that often the most important "therapy" is conducted outside therapy rooms in informal interaction between staff and residents—around the meal table, the pool table, at bedtime, on outings, and when parents visit. While such work is often undervalued, it is crucial since it revolves around the ordinary aspects of everyday life—and it is in everyday life that problems have occurred and solutions will be found.

The challenge is to find a way of thinking about the residential program that gives a framework for *all* the therapeutic work that happens. If clients, therapy staff, child-care or youth work staff, and support staff have a common goal and shared idea about the placement, they can complement each other's work rather than competing. A "theme" for a placement provides a common description of what is being worked upon and common language for talking about it.

The first task in framing the residential placement as a period of transition is the building of a frame or theme that separates the placement from what has gone before and orients it towards a different future. That is, the placement is described in ways that suggest it is a first step in a different view of the future rather than more of the same frustration and failure. This will most often be achieved in some kind of therapy or counseling session at the time of admission. However, in programs that do not involve specific therapy, the process can still occur in the discussions that are inevitably part of a young person entering the program. Even the most apparently uninterested parents will usually agree to a meeting to discuss the practical aspects of their child's placement, and such a meeting can begin the process of people seeing things differently. My experience is that parents' unwillingness to be involved may usually be understood as reflecting their feelings of frustration, failure, and hopelessness and an understandable fear that these will be confirmed. An interview or discussion that seeks to frame things differently may lead to parents becoming more willing to be part of the program. Therapists and residential staff should be wary of "writing off" uninvolved parents too quickly.

Once established, the theme permeates every aspect of the placement—although sometimes more overtly than other times. It is important to note at the outset that the theme is not "sacrosanct." It can change and needs to be flexible. Most importantly, it needs to **fit** with the experience of the family and adolescent.

REFRAMING—A DIFFERENT MEANING FOR THE PLACEMENT

Reframing is an idea well-known in the brief and family therapy field. Resting on the idea that the "meaning" of any behavior or event is not fixed, it involves describing a situation in a different way—a way that gives it quite a different meaning . Watzlawick, Weakland, and Fisch (1974, p. 95) define *reframing* as " . . . to change the conceptual and/or emotional setting or viewpoint in relation to which a situation is experienced and to place it in another frame which fits the 'facts' of the same concrete situation equally well or even better, and thereby changes its entire meaning." A different meaning or frame offers people an opportunity to make sense of their experience differently and so to have the option of behaving and feeling differently. In the residential situation, our aim is to describe the residential admission and the circumstances that have led up to it in a way that allows people to make sense of it as being the start of a different future rather than continue to see it in terms of their past failure.

A problem may be reframed in such a way that it then seems more solvable, with the important aspect being not only that the reframe offers a different meaning but that it also "makes sense" to the person involved. I remember a young man who was referred to me for therapy (this was not a residential situation) with a letter from his doctor, which described his problem of "depression and pathological social withdrawal." This was clearly a serious problem, which involved his inability to talk to people in social situations and his feelings of despondency about his failure and the lack of success in interaction. Not being sure how to treat "depression and pathological social withdrawal," I talked with him about his "shyness problem." This description made sense to him, since it fit with his experience of social difficulty and embarrassment. However, it was a description that implied a more normal rather than pathological difficulty. The description did not change the extent of his experience of difficulty (had my description seemed to underrate the seriousness of his difficulties, it would not have fit with his experience); however, it allowed a very different way of thinking about his situation. Specifically, it allowed me to explore *exceptions* to his difficulties. Had I asked him about times that he did not suffer "depression and pathological social withdrawal," he might have found it hard to think of such times. A description in terms of serious pathology would not have allowed him to see the possibility of things being different sometimes. However, he was able to begin to think about times that he had been able to talk to people despite his shyness, and so we were able to begin to build a picture of a solution. It is important to note that neither "depression and pathological social withdrawal" nor "shyness" were the *true* meaning of his condition. He and I could, in essence, agree to call it one or the other as long as both fit his experience. "Shyness" was a description that gave us both some possibilities for moving forward.

Residential placements are often framed in ways that highlight feelings of failure. As I have described in the first chapter, families (particularly parents) often see a residential admission as a last attempt to have their child "fixed." This frame is inevitably counterproductive, coming as it does from feelings of failure and desperation, and even a successful placement may be further disempowering. The process of building a theme for a placement is a process of reframing the nature and aims of the placement. Our aim in constructing the theme is to offer a meaning frame that allows people to see the placement and the future differently. If they can see it differently, they may be able to see the possibility of different behavior and interaction.

COMMON DESCRIPTIONS OF
RESIDENTIAL PLACEMENTS

I have often heard parents exclaim "we need a break." I have also witnessed residential programs that offer to provide parents with "a break."

The problem is in thinking about "Why do these parents need a break?" While we might try to think of a break as fairly neutral, it is hard to escape from the fact that needing a break is easily seen as evidence of failure. A residential program may seem benign in offering parents and child a break, but the fact remains that most parents do not need a hospital or agency to give them a break from parenting. Hence, no matter how supportive and understanding a residential program may be, it is hard for parents to think about needing a break without making sense of it in terms of having failed as parents.

A residential program that offers a break may be successful, yet parents may be further disempowered, and so the view of themselves as incompetent will be perpetuated. Not surprisingly, they are likely to continue to behave in ways that fit with this view, and so might do or say things that will be interpreted as "sabotaging the placement" or "rejecting the child."

Sometimes, the meaning of a placement for parents is even more explicit. "Take our child and fix him" is a reasonable summary of the attitude of many parents who are at the end of their tether. In the light of their efforts to manage the situation and their continued feelings of failure, this is understandable. Nonetheless, this frame does not make it likely that they will respond to evidence of success, for the program's success might confirm their previous failure.

How do children and adolescents make sense of a residential placement? For many of them, they have had the experience of their parents threatening to "send them away." Even if the residential program is fun in itself, I am sure that young people often make sense of their admission either in terms of "my parents are throwing me out" or "there must be something wrong with me." Neither of these offer much hope.

BECOMING A FAMILY SLOWLY

Anna and Sophie, 13 and 15, had lived with their mother for a number of years since their parents' divorce. They saw Dad regularly; however, it was clear to them that he was enjoying the single life. Things went well until their mother became seriously ill and died. As well as coping with the grief at the loss of their mother, they suddenly found themselves living with their father. They had spent weekends with him, yet living with him full-time was very different.

Dad was not used to caring for two teenage girls, and conflicts soon developed. The girls felt that Dad was unreasonable in his demands on them, and he became increasingly frustrated at their lack of cooperation with him. Arguments escalated, the girls spent increasing amounts of time not coming home, and Dad resorted to increasingly punitive attempts to manage their behavior.

The State welfare department became involved as school personnel worried about whether the girls were being adequately cared for. Dad readily agreed that he had no control over his daughters, and they were placed in a residential program. They performed well in the program and returned home; however, it was not long before the situation deteriorated again. Two further placements were tried, including a foster placement. These placements all seemed to go well — the girls' behavior seemed to settle and people felt that they were ready to go back to living with Dad. Unfortunately, on each occasion, things went well for a while before Dad began complaining again that the girls were not fitting in, and were being uncooperative and defiant.

There were various ideas suggested to explain this situation, including that the girls were still grieving their mother's death, or that Dad was incapable of looking after two adolescent girls. None of these explanations provided a way forward. All the placements, though well-meaning, had been framed in ways that allowed both father and adolescents to feel that other people were seeking to "fix" the problem and that they were little more than subjects or bystanders.

When the family was referred to yet another residential program, the therapist working with them decided to frame the situation differently — to frame it in a way that would allow both Dad and the girls to experience themselves as having some input into the situation. The therapist, after having listened to father and the girls and having gained some understanding of how difficult the situation had been (importantly, having validated their experience of frustration and failure), suggested that one way of looking at their problem was that they had not had control over their coming back together. Other people had decided when they were ready to come together as a family. Perhaps this had rushed things — what was important was that they had not been able to make these decisions for themselves. Since they had not been a family before, how could anyone expect them to be a family if they were not able to have control over the process of becoming a family? Maybe they needed to come together more slowly?

The family was offered a residential placement for the girls, with the aim of the placement being that they could all have some practice in figuring out how to be a family and have control over coming together at their own pace.

It is fruitless to argue about whether or not this explanation is "true." It was one possible way of making sense of the situation. What was important was that it seemed to make sense to the girls and their father, and it offered the possibility of them experiencing themselves as having some control over what was happening to them.

The girls were admitted so that they could practice figuring out how to be part of a family with Dad. During the admission, various behaviors were highlighted as being the kinds of things that would help the family move forward together. Other behaviors were described as trying to do one's own thing—which may be fine, but does not help move towards being a family. This made sense, because it was apparent that the girls really wanted to be part of a family with their father. It was just that they, and he, did not know how. Thus the theme allowed "problem behavior" to be seen in the context of their goal rather than simply as unacceptable according to some arbitrary criterion.

It was clear that the period of the girls' admission was also a chance for Dad to figure out what being a Dad meant, and to practice this. His practice involved both reorganizing aspects of his life and practicing being a dad when the girls came to him on weekend leave.

Staff dealt with the girls' behavior in various ways and sometimes had to impose punishments or consequences for infractions of the rules. However, such infractions were discussed in terms of it being under-standable that the girls had become used to managing their own behavior and that becoming subject to adults would take some practice. Staff made an effort to highlight any behavior that was more cooperative or considerate, wondered aloud how the girls were able to manage this, and discussed with them how such behavior might make a difference when they returned to Dad. It was common for staff to ask, "How will you know when you are ready to be a family again?" and to invite the girls to consider any incident in terms of whether or not it helped them know they were ready to be a family with Dad.

In family sessions, the therapist and residential staff reviewed the girls' achievements and asked them and Dad whether these were things that helped them feel ready to be a family again. Dad's thoughts and plans were also reviewed in terms of his practicing or preparing to be a father to these girls. Therapist and residential staff were careful never to suggest that the girls might be ready for discharge. Rather, the family was often asked when they thought they would be ready, and how they would know when they were ready.

In one family session, the girls presented their father with a gift. He unwrapped the gaudy, brightly-colored paper to discover a wild, ostentatious tie. Dad swallowed his distaste at this fashion disaster and thanked his daughters for the gift. They chorused, "Great, Dad, that was a test in how good you are at being a Dad—and you passed the test!"

Weekend visits home were not without problems, but the theme that had been developed allowed every incident to be responded to in terms of "practicing being a family again." Successes were noted. Things that did not go so well were still examples of practice and could lead to discussions about what could be done differently — without implications of blame or fault.

Finally, weekend visits home were extended by more and more days, and the girls were discharged into father's care. Importantly, they were always given control over the decisions about increased time at home. Follow-up therapy sessions showed that the family experienced further difficulties, yet they seemed better prepared to face these together.

—Robinson House, Care Force Youth Services, Sydney

In this case, the family had experienced other people—"experts"—deciding when it was right for them to get together. The context of this placement was one that allowed them to feel that they had control over the process. They were asked to make decisions about time at home and about discharge, a process that not only allowed them control but also reaffirmed that they were the experts who were in the best position to make these decisions. Staff attempted to respond to everything that happened in terms of the theme, thus giving the placement some coherence and keeping it focused on the family's goal. When they decided they were ready to reunite as a family, the fact that they had experienced themselves as having control over this made it more likely they would be successful.

ALTERNATE DESCRIPTIONS OF PLACEMENT

This example shows the important aspect of themes that provide a different description of the residential placement.

1. The theme must make sense to the family members.
2. The theme provides a different description of the situation, which gives it a different meaning and so counters the previous sense of hopelessness.
3. The theme is framed in a way that maximizes the family members' sense of having control over their own destiny.
4. The theme provides a framework and a language for staff and family to use during the placement.
5. The theme is "goal-directed" rather than "problem-driven."

6. The theme not only sets the goals for the child or adolescent, but also provides a way for parents to be part of the process of change.

Beyond these principles, themes are not "magic." At times, they will be described in obviously creative, even "catchy" ways. At other times, they will seem ordinary. Either way, they must be meaningful. I have had much experience, both in therapy and in residential settings, of devising wonderful-sounding reframes or themes of which I was very proud, which staff saw as raising various creative possibilities, but to which family members did not relate at all. I have heard therapists talk of "getting the family to buy the reframe," which suggests that the therapist has come up with a great idea and now just has to convince the family to accept it. Not only is such an imposition at odds with our aim that family members should experience themselves as experts in the process, it also rarely works.

THEMES ARISING FROM A FOCUS ON SUCCESS

If our aim is that residents will be able to experience themselves as competent and successful, it makes sense that we should try to harness success that has already occurred. No matter how overwhelming their problem history may seem, we can almost always find "exceptions" to the problem.

> Exceptions are those behaviors, perceptions, thoughts and feelings that contrast with the complaint and have the potential of leading to a solution if amplified by the therapist and/or increased by the client. (Lipchik, 1988, p. 4)

The foundation of solution behavior is the idea of *exceptions*—that is, there are already examples of successful or solution behavior (exceptions to problem behavior) that exist in the person's repertoire and that provide the basis for building on; however, the person may not notice these or may not think them important. One of the main tasks of solution-focused therapy is to identify these exceptions and invite the person to consider them meaningfully, since they provide the basis for a new view of self as competent.

Examples of success may seem to pale into insignificance in the light of a history of failure, but we may be able to highlight and build a theme around them. This kind of theme has the advantage of framing the residential placement as building on something that is already happening or doing "more of the same that works." This is a more positive, and achievable, goal than one of "working on a problem."

   Andy, 36, was a long-term alcohol abuser, constantly involved with the law due to alcohol-related incidents.* Andy reported that he was so well-known to the police as a drunk that they would stop him just to see him sober. Although his parole officer had allowed Andy to make his own choice about seeking treatment, her recommendation had been detoxification followed by a 28-day residential treatment program, and it is unclear whether or not Andy experienced himself as really having a choice. Andy had no previous treatment history before being referred to the short-term residential crisis intervention and substance abuse detoxification service.

   It was clear that the police were not the only people who expected Andy to be drunk and in trouble, and Andy felt overwhelmed by everyone's expectations of him. Maybe they were right. Maybe he was a hopeless case. Nonetheless, Andy stated that he wanted to put his reputation behind him — a challenging task because his whole family shared this reputation. While putting his reputation behind him was what he wanted, it was hard for him to feel capable of achieving this. It was hard for him to imagine that he could have any control over how other people saw and treated him.

   In staff discussions with Andy, an exception to his drunken history emerged and proved the key to his goal becoming attainable. Since his arrest, he had been sober. When asked how he could account for the fact that someone with his history could stay sober for four months with only two "hiccups," Andy suddenly brightened and became cooperative and involved during the remainder of his residential treatment. He was encouraged to think about how his successful period of not drinking might have affected his reputation. "Putting his reputation behind him" became the theme for his placement, and his various activities were then framed as practicing doing things that would help other people see him differently. In this way, he could begin to have some control over his reputation.

   As Andy's program built upon this exception, his success was the springboard for his parole officer agreeing that outpatient treatment might be more appropriate for Andy. Andy successfully detoxed and developed a plan for outpatient treatment and getting a job. At last

---

*The major focus of this book is on residential treatment of children and adolescents and most of the examples reflect this focus. Nonetheless, the ideas may also have application in adult residential settings, including psychiatric and substance abuse programs, and so I have also included a number of examples from an adult program.

contact he was temporarily living with an AA sponsor, had entered outpatient treatment, and was still sober.

— Prince William County Mental Health Services
Crisis/Detox Program, Manassas, Virginia

The theme, "putting his reputation behind him," arose from Andy's own words about his situation and so was more likely to make sense to him than a theme invented by the therapist. The discovery of an exception, which he had not previously seen as significant, was able to be related to this theme and made it meaningful to him. Without this, the theme might have provided a new way of talking about his program but might not have been different in its meaning for Andy. That is, it might not have been a description that allowed him to experience himself as having some control over achieving his goal.

The theme provided a way for everyone involved to see things in a consistent way. Staff could look out for any examples of Andy's behavior that might be framed as part of putting his reputation behind him. Whenever they responded in these terms, it would allow Andy not only to receive acknowledgment for a success (however small), but also to see it as part of the process of reaching his goal.

In the following chapter is a more detailed example of the process of developing a theme based upon small successes or competencies that could be identified as already occurring.

Externalizing Problems

Part of what is so overwhelming about the kinds of problems children, adolescents, and their families present is that problems are often thought of as being "part of" the young person. It is common for families, and professionals, to talk about people as if the problem was the person. Parents and young people may see the problem as illness, part of the personality, or as "he's just like that." To the young person, this may interpreted as "I am the problem."

I remember working in the pediatric department of a hospital and dealing with a number of young people who suffered from asthma. Some of them *were* asthmatics. If you asked them, they would say "I am an asthmatic." Others were children or adolescents who happened to have life-threatening asthma. That is, they did not appear to define themselves in terms of their asthma, even though it was no less serious than that of the first group. It was often this latter group who seemed better able to monitor their own medication and feel some control over their lives, and often the first group who seemed to need looking after. The first group had a view of themselves in which the illness was an integral part. The second group seemed to have been able to treat the asthma *as if* it were something separate, something external, and their view of themselves allowed the possibility of doing something about the asthma.

"Externalizing the problem" is a form of reframing that harnesses this kind of distinction. Suggested by White (1984, 1986, 1989), it involves framing the problem as though it were an external entity that is dominating the family members. By framing it in this way, family members may be able to see the possibility of acting on the problem, controlling it, or doing something about it. The reframe sets the stage for contrasting the problem's effects on people with those times they have successfully "stood up to it." Framing the problem as external cuts across the cycles of guilt and blame that usually accompany more internal descriptions, and parents and child (and residential staff) can join together against the problem rather than being against each other. Epston (1991) has distinguished between "externalizing" and "personifying" the problem. Particularly when working with children, they will often respond to the idea of the problem as a tyrant or monster, described as if it had personality characteristics, against which they may fight.

I have described elsewhere (Durrant, 1987) a 14-year-old who had been sexually abused in the past and displayed various "bizarre" sexual behaviors. The description of these as "habits" that were trying to take over his life made sense to him, and he responded well to thinking of the habits as getting angry as he took control over them. "Habit fighting practice" was the theme for his placement initially and allowed him to see the possibility that he could take some control over what he had felt to be part of him, evidence of some damage about which he could do nothing. Given his view that the sexual abuse had "caused" his problems and would probably lead to him becoming an abuser or a pervert, his success over the habits was described as "standing up to the Past." "The Past" was externalized, but not personified, and this broader theme allowed other evidence of his control over different aspects of his life to be highlighted.

Externalizing the problem can be a useful foundation for a theme for a placement, particularly if clients seem unable to identify successes or exceptions, or if the young person and the staff prefer a more "structured" framework for the placement. It is an approach that may work particularly well with younger children. It can also provide a good way to involve parents, as they join with their child against the problem.

In the early development of the ideas about residential treatment presented in this book, externalizing was probably for some time the most frequently used basis for building a theme. My own experience is that it may sometimes be a useful approach, although my preference would be to build a theme on the basis of successes that are already occurring. There are a number of aspects of themes based on externalizing reframes of which staff should be careful. First, while externalizing the problem provides a very different way of talking about the problem, one that may allow family members to see themselves as being able to do something about the problem, it is still a frame that focuses on the problem rather than one that focuses on solution or success. If a theme based on externalizing allows staff, young person, and family members to focus primarily on successes in standing up to the problem, it can be very helpful. If, however, it maintains a focus on the problem, it may be unhelpful. In the example above, "fighting habits" and "standing up to the Past" were useful because they allowed a focus on the times when the boy was successfully doing these things. As the placement proceeded, the theme was broadened to one of "practicing growing up" as a way of building on successes that had been described by the boy himself as being "more grown up." It was important that the focus of the theme move away from the (externalized) problem focus to one based more on ideas of competence. A second concern is that the externalized frame may easily promote too great an emphasis on the young person's "struggle against the problem" without including parents in the task other than as observers or supporters. It is important to include parents as active participants in the process.

Peter (12) was admitted to the short-term residential unit as an emergency admission following a "blow up" at home. Peter lived with his mother, Susan; his brother (15) was serving a period of juvenile detention.

Mother complained that Peter had a violent temper, over which he seemed to have little or no control. She said that this had been a problem for years, but had become particularly bad in the last 12 months. She had resorted to belting him as the only way she could deal with his behavior. She had tried other solutions such as talking, shouting, and grounding him. She was very afraid of what he might do next, as he had recently threatened her with a knife during an argument.

Peter was reluctant to speak during the interview following his admission except to contradict his mother and to accuse her of being unreasonable. However, he did acknowledge that he had a temper problem and responded to some questions aimed at determining the influence of this problem in his life. The therapist wondered how long had this been a concern? Had the Temper had the same strength over the years, or had it changed in its strength? Peter did not know what kinds of things triggered the Temper but said that it had been gaining more and more control over his life, particularly in the last 12 months. In the past week the Temper had taken over three times, and had managed to get him shouting and screaming at his mother.

When asked which other areas of Peter's life had been affected by this problem, they said that although there were some behavior concerns at school, his temper had not taken over there to the same extent, and that the Temper did not come out when they visited other people. The therapist wondered how Peter had managed to retain more control in these areas. This question puzzled them.

Various angry exchanges between the two during the session led to escalation of hostility. They seemed stuck in a pattern of interaction and had become increasingly unable to break out of this and find a new way of dealing with their problems. Certain beliefs had grown out of this situation and contributed to its maintenance—Peter believed that he could not exert control over this temper; Mother believed that the temper was primarily aimed at her; Peter believed his mother wanted to give him a hard time. These beliefs were preventing them from finding new solutions, and strengthened ideas that each was deliberately doing these things.

In order to challenge some of these problem-maintaining beliefs, the therapist had begun to refer to "the Temper" in his questions and statements. He suggested to them that this temper not only had been dominating Peter, but also had been pushing Susan's life around. This temper had gained much strength over the years and was now tyrannizing them both. It was not surprising that Peter felt that it had a lot of control, or that his mother's attempts at managing the situation ended in frustration. Susan nodded a couple of times as this description of events seemed to make sense to her.

The therapist spoke with Peter about whether he wanted to work towards becoming the boss of the Temper, particularly in the light of those times he already seemed to have it under control. The idea that he could do this was new to Peter, and he said he did not realize that he had a choice. The therapist wondered, "How is it that the Temper has tricked you into thinking that you do not have a choice in this?" His mother said she was willing to assist Peter in his struggle with the Temper and agreed to think about what coaching Peter might need in order to become boss of the Temper.

The youth workers in the unit helped Peter in his thinking by reminding him from time to time of the question about becoming boss over the Temper and by keeping a record of times that Peter controlled the Temper. Peter agreed to allowing the youth workers to help him in this way.

Peter also agreed to have the Temper put under some pressure in order to help him work out how difficult it would be to stand up to it. It was agreed that the residential staff would give him six "Temper Control Tests" before the next interview. These tests would involve the staff deliberately putting him in a situation during day-to-day activities where his temper would be tested. Peter agreed to have these tests and was warned that he would not know exactly when they would occur. He would be told whether or not he had passed immediately after each test and agreed to keep a record of the results.

These tests were framed as a way of helping him test his determination and practice taking control. Examples might be telling him to re-do a household chore when he was in a hurry, removing him from an activity for a short time, giving him an extra responsibility, leaving him unsupervised for a short time, saying "no" to a small request, and so on. They would be deliberately planned by staff during normal activities, and not at times that were already "pressured." All would have the common element of providing a small test of his control and with the expectation that he would probably be able to succeed. The tests would be implemented in such a way as to not embarrass or belittle Peter. Peter's agreement to "put himself to the test" indicated that he had some renewed confidence in his ability to control the Temper.

Before the next interview Peter had passed all six of his temper control tests and had been basically cooperative in the unit. The staff noticed that there were times when he had been angry, but had kept control of himself. He had had one fight with another resident. In this, and subsequent interviews, residential staff reported on the successes they had noticed Peter having over the Temper, and his mother was engaged in discussion about how he might have achieved this. As visits home approached, the therapist discussed with Peter's mother how she might respond differently in order to act as his coach. As she described how she characteristically lost her temper at Peter's behavior, she agreed that the Temper had been having some control of her life as well, and visits home became a chance for both to practice control.

Peter left the residential unit after a three-and-a-half months' stay and was given a farewell party to highlight his departure and to mark the entrance into the new phase of his life at home. This celebration, which his mother attended, was a ritual to signify the new context in which the family was in control of their situation. At the party, speeches

were made contrasting the old and the new, Peter was presented with a
Champion Temper Tamer Certificate and his mother with an Expert
Temper Taming Coach certificate.

—adapted from Coles (1986)

Peter's case demonstrates how it was possible to incorporate mother's
part in the interactional process into the theme and how the theme provided a framework for the general responses of staff during the program,
for specific therapy "tasks" for Peter, and for negotiation about such things
as visits home.

*Sally, aged 16, was admitted to the acute care hospital as a result of
suicidal threats, attempted overdose, and basically being out of her
parents' control. Her parents were at their wits' end and exclaimed that
they could no longer "keep an eye on her" all the time. Sally remained
in the hospital for approximately one month before being transferred
to the day treatment program.*

*In exploring the issues the family presented, the therapist suggested
that Sally and her family were under the influence of perfectionism
and thus were required constantly to watch out with a critical eye.
Keeping an eye on a child is part of being a parent; however, it seemed
that the "critical eye" was dominating the family and denying them
choice about how to interact with their growing daughter. Keeping an
eye on oneself, and being conscious of one's emotions and behavior are
part of becoming an adolescent, but the influence of perfectionism was
dominating Sally and making her miserable. Sally was a loyal family
member, and so the tradition of perfectionism made her vulnerable to
the "critical eye."*

*"Escaping the critical eye" became the theme for the program, and it
provided a language for responding to examples of competent behavior.
Both Sally and her family began to recognize the strengths that each had.
To celebrate Sally's successful escape from the "critical eye" when she
was discharged, she was given a magnifying glass symbolizing a tradition
of looking closely at herself and family to find imperfections and a rock to
smash the magnifying glass, thus ending the tradition. This worked very
well, and the last we heard, Sally continued to do well.*

—Shadow Mountain Institute, Tulsa, Oklahoma

The "critical eye" was an externalized description. It was more complex
than the previous example ("the Temper"); however, it fit this family.
Importantly, it provided a platform for highlighting the family's strengths
and allowing them to make sense of these strengths in a meaningful way.

Framing placements or developing themes need not be a complicated process. Whether we are explicit about it or not, any residential placement has some purpose. This purpose will determine how all involved think about what they are doing, how the program operates, and how staff respond to various events. A theme should build on strengths and offer real possibility of change rather than dwelling on a pessimistic focus on the problem.

THE ADMISSION INTERVIEW

It is not important that a "fancy" theme be developed for the placement. Although a theme is very useful, its use is in providing a focus for the residential placement. That is, the theme is not an end in itself. What is important is that the admission begin in a manner that helps it be, and continue to be, focused on solutions and success.

Hence, the admission interview is crucial in that it sets the tone for the interaction between the family and the program. It is preferable that contact with the family begin in the same manner as we hope it will continue. If the admission interview is experienced by family members as a search for pathology and diagnosis, or as a detailed exploration of all facets of the problem, then it may contribute to a focus that is opposite to the competency focus of the rest of the program.

It is tempting to think of "assessment" and "treatment" as separate activities and then to defer treatment considerations until the assessment has been completed. However, if our focus is on meaning and experience, we must remember that the clients will in some way *make sense* of the assessment interview. It is not possible for it to be neutral. They will either make sense of it in a way that strengthens their pessimism, their sense of failure, or their lack of motivation, or they will experience it in a way that encourages greater optimism and helps them to begin to see the possibility of greater competence. Which experience they have will be determined by how we conduct the interview and what kinds of information we focus upon.

Different styles of interviewing will suit different programs. What is important is that the interview enhance the focus on competency. As such, it should seek information about exceptions and successes rather than seek to discover everything there is to know about the previous failure and problem—although, as I have already suggested, clients need to feel that we are validating their experience, and we must be careful to avoid appearing patronizing in the way we explore and respond to information about exceptions and success. In the end it is the clients' acceptance of the significance of the exception that is vital to its success. Many thera-

GUIDELINES FOR ADMISSION INTERVIEW

1. Acknowledge the decision for treatment as reflecting the client's perception, or parents' perception, that they want to do things differently.
2. Using the intake form, ask the following questions: (this example uses "depression" as the presenting problem).
   a. Tell me what you think it would be helpful for me to know about what's brought you here.
   b. When are the times that the depression does not affect you so much?
   c. What will be different when you are ready to leave treatment (get along with your parents, keep your job, save your marriage, etc.)?
   d. What needs to happen with the depression in order to make these differences happen?
   e. Who will notice when the depression is no longer bothering you? What will they notice?
   f. How many days in a week are you not depressed, or less depressed? How many hours in a day are you not depressed, or less depressed?
   g. What are you doing differently at those times?
3. List the exceptions discovered above.
4. Frame the treatment plan with the goals as identified above ("What will be different . . . ," "What needs to happen . . . ") utilizing the exceptions noted.

For example: "Our plan is to end or reduce depression by building on the following activities and strategies (the exceptions) leading to a closer relationship with mother, better control of angry and sad feelings and getting on better at school (the goals), through family therapy, the solution-oriented inpatient program, and participation in the following solution-focused groups. . . ."

© 1992, Linda Metcalf—Adapted with permission.

FIGURE 3.1:   Example of a "Pro-forma" Outline for Admission Interview (Willow Creek Hospital, Arlington, Texas)

pists and workers who have adopted a more competency-based approach find that they require less information than they had previously thought. Certainly, a focus on success does not require detailed *problem* information (and I am certain that we often get detailed information on history and background simply because we feel that it *should* be important rather than because it actually helps us). Figure 3.1 shows an example of guidelines for the admission interview that help focus on specific goals defined in terms of success.

4

PRACTICING HAVING GOOD DAYS: A PLACEMENT "FRAMED"

There is no one "right way" to construct a theme for a placement. The best themes arise from the interactional process that is an interview and employ the words used by the clients. The aim is to establish a theme that builds upon some recognition of the young person and family as having some competence or expertise.

Whether or not a program includes "formal" therapy, there is almost always some kind of interview or meeting to arrange the young person's admission. Even such a less formal meeting may be used to develop some kind of a theme for the placement and so provide a focus or common language for the rest of the placement.

The following is the transcript of parts of a "theme-setting" interview with an adolescent and his family. The transcript is set out here in some detail, to give some idea of the process of building a new "frame" or theme as therapist and family interacted.*

Jeffrey, age 14, who lived with his mother and his 17–year-old sister, Rose, was taken to court after being arrested for stealing and was placed on probation. Two years later, his mother sought a residential placement because she felt that she could no longer manage his behavior. Jeffrey was angry and felt that this was grossly unfair.

---

*The therapist was Michael Durrant, and the interview was a consultation interview in a residential program. Present in the interview was the Senior Youth Worker. Kate Kowalski acted as a "team" for this interview.

FROM PROBLEM TO COMPETENCE

Jeffrey's "unmotivated" stance suggested that a lengthy exploration of his stealing problem would be unfruitful, since this did not seem to be a problem he was motivated to "work on." When asked "how come he was here," Jeffrey acknowledged that "stealing is my main problem." It might have been possible to externalize the stealing as something dominating him, but the therapist thought it unlikely that Jeffrey would respond to this. The extent of his sullenness and lack of apparent motivation suggested that any "theme" for his placement based on such an externalization would be precarious. However, seeking to begin in a solution-focused direction, Jeffrey's answer that "stealing is my main problem" might be framed as evidence of his being honest.

The therapist's assumption was that Jeffrey's feeling that his placement was unfair reflected a sense that things were happening to him over which he had no control. Not only had his behavior reflected a degree of "out-of-controlness," but he was now in a system that he experienced as taking all the control and leaving him little opportunity to experience any competence. Rather than focus on his stealing, the therapist began from the outset to seek "exceptions"—any signs of his competence or control—and build a theme on those.

Therapist: *(to Mother)* How do you see things? How do you see the process that led up to Jeffrey coming here?

Mother: Well, I was getting afraid. It was getting to the point where I couldn't handle him any more. No matter what I did, he just got out of hand. With my being a single parent it was hard. As long as I was there at home with him, one-on-one, he was a good boy, but the minute I had to go back to work he just did things. As long as I was home and didn't work, he was a good boy. He's the type of boy you've got to be one-on-one with. . . .

Therapist: So you were really clear that something had to happen to make things change.

Mother: No matter what I did, I took him to different doctors and we were in counseling, I'd sit there in counseling with him no matter what. He gave me a lot of problems in school and I would try to stick up for him. . . . I know I was wrong, but a child has got to feel like you're on their side. I was always there for him. And I know I was wrong but I wanted to stick up for him. But it didn't work, so I just turned him over to the court, let them try to help him.

It was clear that Mother felt an enormous burden of responsibility for the situation. She had carried the load of Jeffrey's upbringing on her own and was now feeling guilty about how things had turned out. It would be important for the therapist to bear in mind the need to validate her concerns and consider the extent to which she was taking all the responsibility for a solution to Jeffrey's problems.

Therapist: Jeffrey, you've been here two weeks and you don't think it's fair . . . I'm really interested that you're able to be so straight with me. You said, straight out, "I steal things." I've seen guys, and I ask them what the problem is or how come they're here, and they just say, "Oh, I dunno!" How come you're able to be so straight about it?

Jeffrey: *(silence)*

Mother: Is it the way I raised you? I always told you to be honest.

Therapist: Is being honest something that's important to you?

Jeffrey: Yes.

Therapist: You probably know guys who say, "I don't know what the problem is . . . it's unfair, I didn't do anything," but, straight off, you're able to say, "Yeah, I steal, I stay out late." Do you have any ideas about how come you're able to be so straight?

Jeffrey: Well, I did it.

Therapist: *(to Rose)* Do you think Jeffrey generally is pretty straight about things, honest about things?

Rose: Yeah.

Mother: Sometimes he exaggerates.

Therapist: You don't think he's exaggerating when he tells me he's been stealing?

Mother: No. Although what he does is, he always gets caught. Some kids can be a thief and get away with it, but he always gets caught.

Therapist: Do you need more practice in being a thief?

Jeffrey: No.

Therapist: Maybe, being here, you could learn how to do it without getting caught.

Jeffrey: *(laughs)*

Therapist: *(to residential worker)* You must have had other kids here who say, "I didn't steal, I don't do anything wrong." You know, who don't seem to be able to take responsibility for what's got them here. Have you had guys here like that?

Worker: Yes, we have had quite a lot like that.

Therapist: So, I'm really impressed that Jeffrey is able right up front to say, "This is why I'm here, this is what I've done."

Jeffrey's response of "Stealing is my main problem" was hardly a statement of remorse, yet it was something that could be framed as honesty and openness—hence an exception in the prevailing view of him. The interchange about "learning to be a better thief" is lighthearted, but is designed to offer Jeffrey the opportunity to argue for change himself.

Therapist: And how long to you think you're likely to be here?

Jeffrey: Until I'm through with the treatment.

Therapist: Do you have any idea how long that will be?

Jeffrey: Three months.

Therapist: Who will decide, what will determine how long the treatment takes?

Jeffrey: My behavior.

It was quite possible that Jeffrey was just repeating what he had heard. We might well imagine that people had said to him, "Getting out of here depends on you," and had done so as a form of lecture or as a way of haranguing him. Nonetheless, his clear desire to get out and his "recognition" that this depended on him left open the possibility of framing this as his having some control over the process—and might provide a platform for exploring other evidence of control.

Therapist: So getting out of here sort of depends on you a lot.

Jeffrey: Yes.

Therapist: And, Mr. Rolf, you told me that sometimes kids are here for a lot longer than three months.

Worker: Yeah.

Therapist: But Jeffrey, you're saying that you think you'll be able to get out of here in about three months. Do you think in three months that your behavior is going to be showing that you're ready to get out of here?

Jeffrey: Yes.

Therapist: You're pretty confident about that. . . . Say on a scale of zero to ten, where zero is "I don't know if I can do it, I don't know if I'll get out of here at all" and ten is "I really know that I can get my behavior together and get out of here." How confident are you? Where would you put yourself on that scale?

Jeffrey: I'm not sure.

Therapist: Are you real confident, or not confident, or half and half?

Jeffrey: Real sure.

Therapist: So, 7 out of ten . . . or 8 . . . or 9?

Jeffrey: 8.

Therapist: 8 out of 10? So you're pretty sure. And you said that getting out of here depends on you, so you're pretty confident that you're going to be able to do that.

Jeffrey: Yeah.

Therapist: What helps you be that sure? What do you know about you that makes you say, "Yeah, I know I can do it?" Do you think there's some evidence, when you look at yourself, that helps you say, "Yes, I know I can do it"?

Jeffrey: Yes.

Therapist: You do? What sort of things about you tell you that?

Jeffrey: (silence)

Worker: What was it you told me the other day about how you know about right and wrong?

Therapist: Is that right, you said you know about right and wrong?

Jeffrey: Yes.

Therapist: And you're pretty sure you know about right and wrong?

Jeffrey: Yes.

Therapist: So is that something that helps you be confident? You know, you say, "Hey, I know about right and wrong, so I think I'll be able to get my act together and get out of here." Is that one of the things that helps you feel sure?

Jeffrey: Yes.

Therapist: (to Mother) And I guess you'd say you brought him up to know right from wrong?

Mother: I thought I did.

Therapist: So, you've raised him to be honest, and you've raised him to know right and wrong.

Mother: I thought I did.

To try to convince Mother that she was not a failure would be futile. Nonetheless, the therapist was alert for opportunities to challenge gently her view of herself as incompetent.

Therapist: It seems to me that there's some evidence that you've done a pretty good job. Sure, things got a bit off the rails, maybe. But he's been pretty honest with me today. How confident are you that Jeffrey will be able to get his act together and get himself out of here?

Mother: It's got to be what he wants. I mean he was taught what's right and wrong, he's old enough to know what's right and wrong. But he's got to learn for himself. He's got to realize he's not hurting anybody but himself.

Therapist: So are you confident that he's going to be able to do that?

Mother: I really don't know. I don't know how to answer that.

Therapist: So you're cautious.

Mother: I feel like, 'cos I'm by myself, it's more hard for me to deal with than anyone else. I mean I know I'm wrong, but. . . . You know I blame myself for some of the problems he goes through. But I miss him at home. I miss him real bad. He was my little right-hand man.

FURTHER EVIDENCE OF COMPETENCE

When family members are overwhelmed by the enormity of the situation and their own feelings of incompetence, it is hard for them to recognize any deviations from problem behavior. It is often their asides, or quietly spoken comments, that provide the source of exceptions to problem behavior. Mother's statement that she missed Jeffrey, and that he had been her "right-hand man," suggested a possible source of evidence for his competence.

Therapist: Really?

Mother: Yes, he would help take the garbage out, cut the grass, and if something needs fixing, he'd always know how to do that.

Therapist: Really?

Mother: If a light would go out or a light switch don't work, he'd love to fix that. He would know the hot wires and the dead wires. I mean I wouldn't know anything about it but he would. He was very helpful around the house.

Therapist: *(to Jeffrey)* So there have been some ways that you've been able to be pretty helpful and pretty responsible. Since I guess when you're doing something like fixing a light switch, you've got to be pretty careful and sensible, haven't you?

Jeffrey: Yes.

Therapist: So there's some ways that you've been able to be sensible and responsible. Can any of you think of any other ways that Jeffrey has been sensible and responsible and grown up? Since it sounds like there are ways he's been grown up.

Mother: He will talk to me about things. I mean he wants to be grown up. Sometimes I think that . . . well, [Rose is] older and she gets away with some things that he can't get away with, it's always been that way. I always tell him to wait till he gets to that age and then he can do the same things as her. She's 17, she can go out and stay out later than him. But Jeffrey will find a reason to go out and stay out all night. And then he tells me that he fooled with drugs. He tells me that she fools with drugs. But that's not true.

Rose: *(laughs)*

Therapist: What was that?

Rose: He doesn't fool with drugs. He just said that to make her get upset. He will not take drugs. I know.

Therapist: So you're saying he hasn't been fooling with drugs?

Rose: He won't. He ain't stupid.

Again, "He ain't stupid" was an aside, and almost missed. However, it was a comment about the kind of person Jeffrey is. He (and they) might have felt that ending up in a residential facility *was* evidence of being stupid. This was potentially a way to challenge that and to build on the picture of him as competent.

Therapist: What gives you the idea that he isn't stupid?

Rose: I don't think my brother's stupid. He knows right from wrong. He ain't going to mess with drugs. He might steal something, but he don't take drugs.

Therapist: So maybe he's done some dumb things, like stealing maybe, or getting caught, but bottom line is that you know he's not stupid, he's not fooling around with things that are really dangerous.

Rose: The only drugs he takes are what the doctor prescribes, and even then he doesn't like it.

Mother: He will fool with alcohol, though.

Rose: Yes, he will fool with alcohol.

Therapist: So, is that right Jeffrey, you haven't been fooling around with drugs?

Ignoring the "problem-focused" mention of alcohol and sticking with the exception of not fooling with drugs, the therapist wanted to use this revelation as a way of building on the various things that had emerged that were evidence of Jeffrey being competent and in control. This avenue might lead to the notion that he was someone who was capable of showing control and that the residential placement might be framed as a time for practicing regaining that skill. The aim, therefore, was to establish conditions that would allow him to begin to see himself in this way.

A Theme — Good Days Happen Often

Therapist: And Rose thinks you're not stupid. Do you think she's right?

Jeffrey: Yes.

Therapist: So, it's interesting. What strikes me already is that there are a lot of ways in which Jeffrey is pretty grown up and sensible. He was able to be straight and honest with me about things, about what got him here and what he's been doing, he's pretty clear about what he needs to do to get out of here, we've seen that he knows right from wrong, that he's not stupid. Can you see, Jeffrey, why those things make me think "Hey, there's a lot of ways in which this guy is pretty grown up, pretty sensible"?

Jeffrey: Yes.

Therapist: Is that something you think about you? Do you think, "Yeah, I'm pretty grown up, I'm pretty responsible"?

Jeffrey: I think it, but not all the time.

This is probably true. Jeffrey probably *was* able to think of himself as grown up and sensible; however, recent events (both his behavior and the response of the system) would have worked against his remembering that aspect of himself.

Therapist: Okay. What are the times that you do?

Jeffrey: When I'm having a good day.

Therapist: How often do you think you have a good day?

Jeffrey: They happen often.

Therapist: Okay. Do you think other people notice when you have a good day? Are other people able to say, "Hey, Jeffrey's being pretty grown up and responsible today"?

Jeffrey: They know when I'm having a good day.

Therapist: And having a good day is what you prefer?

Jeffrey: Yeah.

Therapist: So, is what you want to get out of being here is to practice giving yourself more good days?

Jeffrey: Yes.

The term "good days" had come from Jeffrey and the best words for establishing themes or "frames" for a placement are the words used by clients. At this stage, "good days" is not a term rich with meaning; nonetheless, it is a summary for those times that Jeffrey is behaving in ways that might be considered grown up and responsible. "Good days" probably also includes days when he is not stealing, yet this is not explicit and does not need to be.

The important thing is that Jeffrey had begun the interview as "a boy with a stealing problem." Potentially, he is now "a boy who has good days most of the time," and this is a description with very different implications. Beginning to think about the theme for the placement as "practicing giving yourself more good days" meant that the residential placement could be seen as Jeffrey working on something he was already able to do, rather than as a time for other people to fix his problem.

The therapist was interested in a clearer idea about what a "good day" is like and asked what was different. Mother's reply was, "I be there, I be at home," and her feeling of responsibility emerged again. The therapist's concern about this was both that it left her feeling the load of ensuring good days, and potentially undermined the thought that Jeffrey could do something to make good days happen. However, she was able to reply to a question, "Are there ever any times when he has a good day when you're not there?" and this led to a discussion about what Jeffrey does differently to give himself good days. (In the light of the assumption that exceptions *do* occur, it might have been better to ask, "When was the last time he had a good day when you were not there?" Such a question, which presupposes competence, is more likely to elicit a further exception.)

MOTHER'S PART IN THE THEME

The theme of "good days" has begun to be established, and these are defined as Jeffrey being "grown up" and "responsible." Mindful of Mother's tendency to feel guilty and responsible, the therapist was interested in exploring her role in the pattern of interaction. She might be taking more than her share of responsibility for the solution to the problem, and her efforts to do this might actually work against Jeffrey assuming more responsibility for his own behavior. Cade (1988) suggests that parents' working harder and harder on their adolescent's behavior may lead to the adolescent working less and less hard. So, Mother working harder and harder to keep Jeffrey out of trouble might have contributed to his taking less responsibility for his own behavior. At the same time, the issue of when to take control and when to "back off" is one that is fraught with anxiety for parents.

Therapist: I was wondering if there were times, when Jeffrey is not having a good day, that you feel like you have to be more responsible for him, you have to keep him out of trouble? I mean, you've said you feel like you should stay home and keep him out of trouble.

Mother: Yes, well there was one time when he went out and got a job at a grocery store, and I felt like this was really good for him. And I told him to come in and go to bed so he could get up for his job the next morning. But he would stay out late, beyond twelve o'clock, and I told him that he would be responsible to make sure he got up to go to this job. And then it fell through, just like I told him. I left him to sleep, and he lost his job.

Therapist: So you decided you weren't going to take responsibility for that, he just had to . . .

Mother: Figure it out for himself.

Therapist: And that's hard. I know it's hard to say, "He's got to figure that out for himself." I guess there are times when you feel like you've got to get in and be responsible.

The therapist was genuinely impressed with Mother's allowing Jeffrey to sleep in and lose his job. She had probably seen his getting a job as a positive move, and it would have been both easy and understandable if she had worked hard to ensure that he got up in time to go to work.

Later in the interview, Mother was asked if she would be interested in using the time of Jeffrey's placement as an opportunity to get some help in figuring out how to let him "figure things out for himself" more. That is, her involvement was discussed, and an agenda set for further work. This was important in that it meant that the placement was a time for both Jeffrey and Mother to practice.

PRACTICAL IMPLICATIONS OF THE THEME

As the interview proceeded, other examples emerged of times that Jeffrey had behaved in more responsible ways and had given himself good days, and of times that he had had bad days. It seemed that the interview had established Jeffrey's ability to have good days and that this was a possible theme for the placement. Importantly, this idea had emerged from Jeffrey and was something for which he appeared to be "motivated."

It seemed that the idea of "practicing giving yourself more good days" was a viable theme for the placement, and that this could involve the idea that Mother might practice allowing Jeffrey to "figure things out for himself." Jeffrey had been admitted for help with his stealing. He was not overly interested in such help, and this description of the situation left little option for his Mother other than to wait for the "experts" to solve the problem that she had been unable to solve.

Harnessing his desire to "get out" and elaborating on what he knew he needed to do to achieve that, as well as the evidence from other parts of his life that he was capable of achieving that, allowed a different picture of Jeffrey to be drawn which fit for him. Seeking to build upon evidence of his competence (and therefore of the real possibility of solution) provided a "platform" for gently challenging Mother's view of her failure. Previously, she carried the burden of a sense of failure and so either had to try to prove her competence or would remain uninvolved with the placement. Highlighting those ways in which Jeffrey had a background of control and a future of more good days—that is, beginning from what he was *already* doing well, rather than from some idea of what he *might* achieve—made it easier for Mother to acknowledge a degree of competence and maximized the likelihood of her feeling involved. For her, the prospect of continuing to practice figuring out when to take over and when to back off is less threatening than the thought of working out what she has been doing wrong! Both Jeffrey and Mother had a way of making sense of the three months they were facing that allowed them to feel some part of that process—even some control over it.

In terms of the pragmatics of the placement, there might be a number of ways to incorporate the focus of the theme. The staff of the unit might build upon the theme by allowing Jeffrey opportunities to monitor and control his own behavior (as opposed to their seeing their role as taking control). They could ask Jeffrey to predict his good days and bad days, or ask him from time to time whether this was to be a good day or a bad day. On days he nominated as "good days," they might allow him more opportunities to behave independently. On other days, they would make it clear that they would work to keep him out of trouble—not punitively, but in recognition of the fact that he might not yet be up to giving himself good days all of the time.

It would be important not only that they give him greater responsibility on good days but that they experiment with giving him such responsibility as a way of achieving good days. That is, greater responsibility should not primarily be a reward for having good days but should be a way of practicing, since it will only be by his experiencing himself as taking greater responsibility that Jeffrey will be able to give himself more good days. It is also important that the staff not use the language of the theme to "push" Jeffrey towards responsible behavior. I discuss at length, in Chapter 10, the importance of residential staff "not working too hard."

Mother's involvement would be in terms of reviewing her ideas about allowing Jeffrey to figure things out for himself, practicing that on times of weekend leave, and encouraging her to notice examples of his keeping himself out of trouble and giving himself more good days.

Of course, this was only an initial interview, which established a theme that might be a "platform" on which the rest of the placement could be built (and, since this was a "consultation interview," the therapist in this case had no control over how the rest of Jeffrey's placement was handled). The interview is not enough, in itself, to ensure that the placement proceeds in a way that is focused on developing competence. That is, developing a theme is not necessarily sufficient—it would be quite possible to do so and then continue with the placement within an essentially problem-focused framework. It will be important that all those involved in a placement such as Jeffrey's plan carefully how they will employ the theme and its focus in the program.

5

SETTING GOALS: THE

FUTURE in the PRESENT

Any program that has a therapeutic focus usually has some notion of the goals for the young person and family concerned. It is clearly my suggestion that these goals ought to give some focus to the entire program, with everything that happens being directed towards their achievement. Unfortunately, this is not always the case. It is all too easy for the goals to be something that are considered in therapy sessions and when reviewing a resident's overall progress, but which get lost at other times in the demands of the day-to-day activities.

"What do you want to work on?" vs.
"Where are you heading?"

The way goals are framed can have a profound bearing on how the placement proceeds. In particular, the goals can either underpin the focus of the placement or work against the placement being framed in a way that facilitates the development of views of competence.

Commonly, goals represent a problem focus. They are framed in terms of "what (problems) the person wants to, or needs to, work on," "what issues need to be addressed," "what behaviors we need to change," and so on. That is, the goals typically relate to getting rid of some problem or changing some problem situation. No matter how benignly they might be expressed, goals framed in these ways may easily contribute to the placement being focused on the problem. I have discussed in Chapter 2 the way that a continued focus on the problem does not necessarily assist with developing a sense that things can be different for the child or adolescent, for the parents, and for the staff.

Rather than focusing on what needs to change or be changed, it may be more helpful to focus on what the changed state will be like — that is, to focus on the nonproblem future. Rather than the program being driven by ideas about changing whatever problem led to the placement, we might orient the placement towards what things will be like when the young person is ready for discharge.

This is more than just a different way of phrasing things. Focusing on what needs to change or be worked on is focusing on the problem with all its difficulty and pessimism. Focusing on what will lead to success is focusing on the solution, and since it implies that success will occur, brings more optimism and direction.

A "rule of thumb," if the placement is a period of practice, is that our focus should constantly be on the resident's discharge. Everything should be framed in a way that looks forward to this.

In discussing therapy, de Shazer (1991) often asks clients, "How will we know when to stop meeting like this?" His emphasis is on the entire therapeutic interaction being oriented towards the "goal state." Everything that happens is judged by how much it allows a move *towards* the solution rather than a move *away* from the problem. This is not just a semantic distinction — it is in the achievement of the goal that lies optimism and feelings of possibility.

In our program, we have developed techniques that help staff and clients be more focused on practicing the changes that are desired. Our first step is known as "the first session summary." This is a form that is completed by the primary therapist or worker, along with the client, at the time of admission. The purpose of this form is to help staff and client focus from the outset on signs that the client is ready for discharge. The form requires the therapist to note any specific symptoms that are being externalized or the theme that has been built, specific language that is helpful to describe the client's viewpoint and goal, and any other information that may be helpful in developing or continuing new frames with the client and family.

The form becomes the major part of the client's file. The main emphasis of the form is on "What will show that the client is ready for discharge?" It provides a way for staff and client to be future-oriented, or solution-focused, from the outset and the rest of the placement seeks to use the information on this form to "look forward" to the client's discharge.

— Prince William County Mental Health Services
Crisis/Detox Program, Manassas, Virginia

The question, "How will you know when you are ready to be discharged?" is not always easy to answer, particularly when people have been feeling dominated by their problems and pessimistic about the future. Nonetheless, it can be a powerful question. Not only does it set the focus firmly on the future, but it implies clearly that the person *will* be ready for discharge at some time and that the person can be the judge of this. It helps set the stage for an approach that encourages our clients to become the experts on themselves.

In an initial therapy session, or an intake meeting, these kinds of questions might be used:

- How will you know when you are ready to leave this program?
- What will you be doing that will tell you that you are ready to go back home?
- When you are ready to move on from here, what do you think people will notice about you that is different from what's happening now?
- If we made a videotape of you now, and then made another videotape of you when you are ready to leave here, what will we see that is different on the second video? How will we be able to tell which is the second video? (The idea of "video descriptions," which encourage specific descriptions of "what will be happening," is discussed by O'Hanlon and Wilk, 1987).
- How will you know when your son/daughter is ready to return home?
- When we get to the point where you are ready to have your son/daughter back home, so you can keep on practicing these things together, what will be different? What will be the signs to you that this time has come?

Not only do questions such as these establish a focus on future success rather than on past failure, they also help the goals be described in concrete terms. They all include the notion, "What will you/he/she *be doing* when things are better?" Vague goals ("We will be getting on better") are hard to measure and hard to achieve. Since we could always find more ways to "get on better together," it is possible that the young person, or the parents, or the staff, may never be confident that the goals have been reached. The more that goals seem ephemeral, the more the person feels like "No matter how much I achieve, there is always another step," and so the more likely it is that clients will give up. de Shazer (1988) points out that concrete goals, which provide a sense of "how we will know when we get there," are an important step towards promoting the possibility of a solution and will often help a family recognize that *some* of what is needed is already happening.

It is then up to us whether the goals become something written in a file and only referred to at formal case reviews, or whether they are used meaningfully throughout the placement. While it is not helpful to belabor them, having the goals as things that are referred to often helps the young person continue to look forward to the future solution. Something that offers a continual, gentle reminder that things *will* get better is the best way to foster "motivation."

MIRACLES CAN HAPPEN IN RESIDENTIAL TREATMENT—IF WE BELIEVE IT!

de Shazer (1988) describes the "miracle question" as an important part of solution-focused brief therapy and as way for establishing goals that are meaningful for the client.

The miracle question is a question of the form:

Suppose one night, while you are asleep, a miracle happens and all the problems that brought you here are solved. How will you know? What will be different that will tell you that the miracle happened? What will your parents notice that will tell them that it happened? (paraphrased from de Shazer, 1988, p. 5)

This question, when pursued, leads to a concrete "picture" of what the solution state will be like. Because it is a "let's pretend" question, it makes it easier for people to answer it without becoming bogged down in the "yes, buts" that reflect their current feelings of hopelessness. It is important to explore the answers to the miracle question, to build up as detailed a picture as possible. It is not uncommon for adolescents initially to respond with something like, "They won't be hassling me all the time." Further questioning might proceed along the lines of, "What will they be doing instead? How will that make a difference to you? So, what will you be doing differently? How will that make things different for you? And for them?" and so on. Similarly, when parents identify the miracle as being,

"He will be doing what he's supposed to do," we may ask, "So, what are the things he will be doing? How will you respond to that? How will that make things different for you? What will he notice that will tell him that you are pleased?" and so on. The aim is to construct a picture or description of the solution state, which is built from a number of specific statements about what all people will be doing differently.

The miracle question can have a number of uses. The very fact of developing this detailed description of the solution seems to have the effect of helping people feel that it is achievable. It is almost as if, as the description of the solution is built, the solution becomes a possibility. "It appears that the mere act of constructing a vision of the solution acts as a catalyst for bringing it about" (O'Hanlon & Weiner-Davis, 1989, p. 106). Again, this is much more likely to lead to "motivation" than is an exploration of all the problems that need to be worked on. Moreover, the behaviors identified as part of the (future) miracle state can then be looked for in the present. Any time that staff, parents, or the young person can notice one of these things already happening, they can feel one step closer to the solution. Finally, the miracle question can provide an agenda for practicing new behaviors, either in the unit or while at home.

Nan, 23, had recently been discharged from an out-of-state psychiatric hospital in the care of her mother. She had been hospitalized after threatening her abusive, alcoholic husband and had been diagnosed as having a major depression. She reported that her mother had been absent a lot during her childhood and had also been physically abusive. She also reported being sexually abused by male relatives.

At the time of her admission, Nan talked about being bothered by critical voices telling her to kill herself. Initially, we thought that practicing management of the voices would be the way we could frame Nan's task. At the second session, Nan persisted in asking what her diagnosis was. We discussed adjustment disorders, noting the succession of stressors she had experienced, culminating in her being hospitalized for attempting to protect herself from her husband. "No wonder she was depressed!" I said, in an attempt to normalize her experience. This discussion shifted her affect and her conversation to one of hopefulness. After stressing that she was already renegotiating family relationships after a stormy adolescence, Nan clearly stated that her goal was to put her past behind her. By the next day, she was planning visits home. After one especially difficult day, we reminded Nan that this was a time of transition, of practice. This was important to normalize the ups and downs that occurred as she practiced new behaviors.

We used the miracle question with Nan, her mother, and her sister as a vehicle for identifying behaviors that would be happening when everything was better, leading to things she could practice while she was visiting home.

When we asked the miracle question, initially the response was, "When she can interact with people without getting angry or hurt and lashing out at people." After some discussion, Nan, her mother, and her sister agreed that signs that the miracle had happened would include Nan spending more time having fun with her sister, her looking for a job, she and her mother enjoying time together, and her continuing to attend church with her stepfather. Nan described that she would know the miracle had happened when she was hearing positive things from her mother. Nan and her mother mentioned that there was a family wedding the next weekend that Nan would be attending. We decided to take advantage of this to encourage Nan to practice being with her family in a different way.

In our therapy sessions and in staff interactions, as we planned leave passes in preparation for the wedding, we talked with Nan about what she would have to do differently to be able to be with her mother and sister in more positive ways. She noted that in order to receive more positive responses she would practice being more positive, both in her thinking and in the way she talked with others. She also said that she was thought about in her extended family as the "crazy daughter" so she decided she would take advantage of that and use it to have fun rather than worrying about conforming or pleasing other family members. In preparation for the wedding, Nan's mother took her shopping for a new dress and fixed her hair for her. Nan looked radiant for the wedding and both had experienced success in their shopping trip.

In a session following the wedding, Nan's mother, without prompting, noted a number of changes in Nan's behavior: Nan had been positive throughout the day of the wedding; Nan had spent time with her sister and both had enjoyed this; and Nan handled a potentially difficult incident in a positive way. The incident had been the result of another family staying at their house for the wedding. Nan had been upset that a young child was being allowed to watch an extremely violent television show. Nan had asked that the child leave the room or that they watch something else. The child's mother objected to this. Nan was briefly upset, but had been able to go on without letting the incident contaminate the remainder of the day.

I asked Nan if she had noticed that she was getting more positive responses from her mother—she beamed as she said, "Yes." When asked what they had to do to continue this progress, both were clear that they had to spend more time together doing family activities and to *spend time alone together in positive ways, something they had not done much of when Nan was a child.*

At last contact before transferring her case to an outpatient program, Nan had survived a week with more miracle days than bad days (in fact one of the bad days had been prescribed). Her mother was beginning to spontaneously report positive changes and Nan had plans to begin a job search the next week.

— Prince William County Mental Health Services
Crisis/Detox Program, Manassas, Virginia

The staff had some ideas about a way of framing Nan's placement, by externalizing her voices; however, this was not what fit best with Nan. Many of us can recount examples of devising a "creative and clever" reframe that, unfortunately, did not fit for the client! "Putting her past behind her" was more meaningful for Nan and flowed from the therapist describing her experience in less pathological ways and highlighting the steps she was already taking to change her relationships with her family. "Putting her past behind her" was meaningful for the client but was not a goal that was readily measurable. That is, there were no ways for knowing when she had achieved this. The miracle question allowed Nan, her family, and the staff to develop a more detailed description of what would be happening when she had achieved this goal. This meant that there were now identifiable things that would show that she was "putting her past behind her," and these behaviors were things with which they could experiment.

WHOSE GOALS?

When young people appear to be unmotivated, it is often the goals that are the problem. We are all most likely to be motivated to work towards goals that we have set and are therefore meaningful for us, and least likely to be motivated to work on goals imposed by someone else. One of the least fruitful activities in which we can engage is to try to convince a young person that he or she has a particular problem. Just because a court, or a school, or a mental health professional, or parents have identified what the problem is and what needs to happen does not mean that the young person will agree.

Within the brief therapy field, several people have described the notion of "customership" for therapy. This idea was introduced by the MRI Brief Therapy Project (Fisch et al., 1982) and has been adapted by de Shazer and his colleagues (de Shazer, 1988). Rather than describing clients in terms of "motivation" or "resistance," this idea suggests that we recognize that clients in different circumstances have a different relationship to therapy and the idea of change. Sometimes, people are "visitors" to therapy (they are often there under duress, not because they wish to be involved, and they may not think that they have a problem at all); others are "complainants" (they acknowledge a problem but feel unwilling, or unable, to try to do anything about it and are not really "motivated" about therapy). Some are "customers" for therapy (they come along wanting help to do something about their situation and are able clearly to articulate how they would like things to be different).

Adolescents referred to residential programs may often be seen as only "visitors"—they do not tend to invite therapists and residential staff to help them change, and they often feel that it is other people (parents, school, police) who really have the problem. However, it is important to note that "customership" (or "visitorship") is not a characteristic of the person but is a way of describing the therapist-client interaction. de Shazer talks of these terms as "code words" and explains that, "the code word 'customer' . . . describes a therapist-client relationship, *as a result of the interview*, that is built on the client's wanting to do something about building a solution" (de Shazer, 1988, p. 42—italics added). That is, a client may be only a "visitor" if the therapist persists with someone else's definition of the problem. As a result of the interview, the therapist and client may have built their relationship around a different definition of the situation—a different agenda—and the client may be a "customer" for that.

In the previous chapter, Jeffrey was only a "visitor" when the interview and the placement were focused on the agenda of his mother and the authorities, his stealing, and his disruptive behavior. By the end of the session, however, he was potentially a "customer" for "having more good days." Of course, as with most adolescents, his "customership" was still tentative.

My experience is that the people with whom we work usually want things to be better. It is just that we must understand what they mean by "better," not what we assume they mean.

Chris was an adolescent who taught us a great deal about the importance of letting go of our hopes and our ideas about goals in order to make room for the young person to develop hopes and goals that were meaningful to him.

Chris had been admitted to the residential program after he had abused a neighbor's daughter. The welfare authorities considered that he could not safely be left at home, since his mother did not think she could supervise him. As well as his involvement in therapy, his program included his attending school outside the unit.

After some months of faultless school attendance, Chris simply stopped going to school. Aware that we should give him choices, we told him he should either return to school, or start looking for work, or enroll in a technical course. These were the usual options for someone in his position. The more we sought to encourage Chris to make a choice, the more he did nothing. We decided to "get creative" and offered further choices — he could return to school, or look for a job, or enroll in a course, or apply for unemployment benefits, or become a bum. Again, he did nothing.

We realized that even our attempts at (supposedly) giving choices was placing pressure on Chris and not really allowing him any sense of control. If he even looked like he might be leaning in any particular direction, it was too easy for us to "jump on" this apparent choice and gently (or not so gently) push him towards it. We were prepared to give him choices, but we were determined he should do something. In fact, as we pushed harder, Chris adopted an almost catatonic role in the unit.

We finally realized that Chris had had lots of experience previously of professionals, agencies, and welfare personnel taking control of his life. He had not really had the opportunity to experience personal agency, and our efforts to have him make a decision were simply, in this context, another example of someone else trying to organize him. Finally, we told him that we would not push him at all and would leave him to make his own decisions. He was expected to comply with the minimum unit expectations, but we would neither chase nor remind him to perform these tasks. Chris was given a stack of business cards with his name on them, and was to leave a card wherever and whenever he decided to carry out a task. These "catch up cards" would allow us to catch up with what he was up to and help prevent us having to chase after him.

As we found his cards, he began doing additional chores and other tasks around the house, thus leaving us extra cards and showing both us and himself that he was organizing himself. We tried to highlight this gently, while still avoiding becoming too enthusiastic about his efforts (since this would have been another way of our interfering).

Eventually, we put aside our expectations about Chris's "choices" and asked him about what his idea was of how things would be when they were the way he wanted. He was very clear that he wanted to be at home with his mother. Other authorities had previously decided that this was not possible; nonetheless, Chris was determined that this was *his wish. Until he was able to work towards this goal, issues such as work or school were peripheral in his mind. As staff concentrated on work vs. school issues, it simply made Chris even more hopeless about his prospects of returning to his mother.*

We had to put aside our ideas about what makes a "successful placement" and find ways to embrace Chris's own goals. Working towards returning home was something about which he was motivated. We talked with him about working to convince his mother (and, by implication, himself) that he was safe to have at home. We assured him that we would provide a safe place in which he could experiment with the things that would be necessary to enable him to return home and that we would be available for advice if he wanted.

When his mother (in response to his inactivity) suspended his allowance, Chris sought advice as to how to apply for a "Jobsearch Allowance," and subsequently accepted our help in finding work. This was important and meaningful to him as part of the process of working on going home, whereas it had not made sense to him when it was simply one of the "choices" we were trying to insist he make.

From that point on, Chris had some focus for his placement—a focus that was meaningful to him rather than one that was imposed by outsiders.

— Trigg Hostel, Care Force Youth Services, Sydney

Even though the staff tried to give Chris as many choices as possible, these choices were still within the framework of other people's goals. Not only were his own goals being ignored, but the "experts" had declared them unattainable. What better way to crush any hope or motivation he might have! If a young person has some idea of how he or she wants things to be, then that is the area that provides the greatest possibility of working cooperatively.

What if the goals are unrealistic? Difficult though it may seem, it is wise not to be too concerned over that question at the outset. In the example above, if Chris's goal was to return home, and this was pronounced unrealistic, then we can expect little more from him than "resistance" or defiance. If, however, we accept this goal and explore it further, we will begin to build a picture of things he might attain. "How will you know when you are ready to return home?" or similar questions, may lead to his specifying particular behaviors or steps towards which he wants to work. For example, getting a job was not a step that was meaningful for Chris until he saw it as part of his quest towards his goal of returning home. The placement may then proceed towards the particular behaviors or achievements that have been identified as characterizing the goal state.

As Chris achieves these, and staff (and his mother, if she is involved) respond to them, he will begin to see himself differently, as being more competent. We can imagine that most of his previous experiences had fostered his view of himself as hopeless, rejected, and unable to exercise much control over the direction of his life. A focus on his steps towards competence and success will aim to help consolidate a different way of seeing himself. Once this has been achieved and Chris is able to view his future through a "lens" of competence and control, discussions about the details of his future might open different possibilities. Within his previous context, going home was the only hope to which he could cling. As he is able to see himself differently, we might then be able to discuss other options. "Now that you have a job and have successfully practiced running your own life, how do you think these things will affect your relationship with your mother? How do you think this will make a difference in the way you relate to other people, such as your neighbor? What will it be like when you continue these things even if you do not end up going back home?" That is, once he has achieved a self-concept of greater success, he is more likely to be able to consider other options.

This example shows both the importance that the goals be the clients' goals rather than ours, and that they be described in specific rather than general terms.

PRACTICING THE FUTURE . . .

The identification of the specific behaviors or activities that will be part of the solution provides useful material for the residential program. In the example above of Nan, the miracle question led to a number of specific behaviors—spending more time having fun with her sister, looking for a job, spending time with her mother, and attending church with her step-father. It was then possible to discuss ways that she might deliberately practice some of these. These activities became steps towards her goal, and each might then be explored to identify the intermediate steps she could practice while in the program. So, for example, talking about possible jobs, looking in the newspaper, practicing writing job applications, perhaps role-playing job interviews, and so on, are all activities that might be undertaken in the program. Because these are derived from the elaboration of Nan's goal, they become meaningful activities rather than just things imposed by staff as being "things you should do."

With children and adolescents admitted because of so-called "behavior disorders," the kinds of changes we might hope they would develop can easily seem like little more than compliance. However, the specific behaviors that are part of the description of the miracle, or part of the answers to "How will you know when you are ready to be discharged" are more likely to lead to positive intermediate steps that might be practiced. Developing a theme such as "practicing controlling your temper" might lead to activities within the program that entail the young person focusing on examples of responding differently to frustration or conflict. Nonetheless, these can still seem contrived or feel like they are primarily ways of complying with staff expectations. However, if various examples of "practicing controlling your temper" have been identified as characteristics of the miracle state, the young person may see it as more relevant that he or she experiment with such responses.

Our aim, when parents are involved, is that they see themselves as part of the process and that the period of their child's residential placement be seen as a chance for them to practice different behaviors or responses. However, if their child is away from home and in the residential unit, it can be difficult for them to see that they can work on responding differently. The answers to future-focused questions can help identify particular things for parents to practice or work on, things that they will be doing differently once the goal has been achieved.

Parents may simply want their child or adolescent to behave differently. Framed this way, it is difficult for them to see that they need to do anything other than wait for their child to change. The kinds of future-focused questions described above can lead to more concrete things for parents to address or practice during the placement. For example, parents might say that the sign of things being better will be that their child is behaving more responsibly. Exploration of how this will make a difference *to them* might lead to such ideas as the parents doing more things together (instead of being completely focused around their child's latest misbehavior), engaging in more pleasant activities with their child, spending less time supervising homework, being more relaxed, and so on. Many of these will provide ideas about activities that parents may practice while their child is in the program. If, for example, they experiment with spending more time together as a couple, or planning things they can do with their child, then these will provide more alternatives when the child finally returns home.

In an example in Chapter 3, part of the way the placement of two adolescent girls was framed was as a chance for Dad to figure out what being a Dad meant, and to practice this. His practice involved both reorganizing aspects of his life and practicing being a Dad when the girls came to him on weekend leave. While it might seem hard for him to practice responding differently while his daughters were in the program, it was possible to identify various ways that *his* life would be different when he was getting along well as the father of these two girls. This involved identifying various specific things that would be different in the way he organized his own life and activities, quite apart from the matter of the way he responded to the girls, and so there were things that he could practice doing differently during the time of the girls' placement.

... OR PRETENDING

Milton Erickson said, "You can pretend anything and achieve it" (Lustig, 1975).

de Shazer (1991) describes a therapy case with clients who had significant psychiatric diagnoses and histories, in which he used the miracle question to construct a picture of the solution state. At the end of the first session, he asked each of them to choose two days during the following week, unknown to the other, and to pretend that the miracle had happened.

As described above, the exploration of the future solution state, using the miracle question or other questions that presuppose change, seems to have the effect of making the solution seem more possible. Once that description has been built, one possibility is to ask the person concerned to "pretend" that it has occurred. It is surprising that people who seem unwilling or unable to practice the steps towards the desired solution will often be quite happy to engage in a pretend task.

> *I once worked with a nine-year-old girl who was in a residential placement following a history of "uncontrollable" behavior. In a therapy session with her parents, we spent quite some time outlining all the things that would be different after the miracle occurred. These were pursued until they were expressed in specific, behavioral terms. I suggested that she choose two days over the following week, while in the residential unit, and pretend that the miracle had occurred. That is, she was to pretend that she did not feel like having tantrums, was having fun, and was not worried about her mother. We had discussed the kinds of things she would be doing when these things happened. The other part of the task was that the residential staff were to try to guess which days she chose as her "pretend days."*

This task has a number of positive aspects. The girl did not really have to *try* to be different, she just had to *pretend* to be different, which is a much less daunting task. The fact that her days were secret, and the staff had to try to guess which days they were, added an element of fun to which she was happy to respond. Finally, even if she did not complete the task, the staff were likely to be on the lookout for different behavior and so were more likely to respond to any examples, however small, of her behaving differently.

After a couple of weeks of the pretending task, which she embraced enthusiastically (since the thought of tricking the staff appealed to her), we were able to institute the same task with her parents during a visit home.

Again, even if she did not deliberately behave differently, her parents were "oriented" to look for different behavior. No matter how terrible her behavior might have been, we can assume that there would be at least one or two small examples of her behaving differently. Given that her parents were looking out for these, they were more likely to notice them and respond to them, thus making it more likely that a different kind of interactional pattern might develop.

6

STRUCTURING the PROGRAM
as ONE of TRANSITION

I remember an interview with a family who had reached "the end of the road." They had made constant efforts to find a counselor who would solve the problems they were having with their son and now sought my help in arranging a residential admission.

"I need to tell you that the youth workers in this program are really terrible at controlling kids' behavior. They are not very good at solving family problems," I warned them.

"However, the youth workers are very good at helping kids and parents practice controlling their own behavior," I said. "We realize that you know more about your own situation than we do, so there is no way we can tell you how things should be in your family. The placement might give you a time with a bit less pressure so you can all practice getting on top of things and practice the things you'll need to do to solve these problems back at home."

Not surprisingly, these parents were a little taken aback at this. They had come hoping that I, and the particular residential program, would be able to "fix" their situation. In terms of their view of the situation, it would have been more comfortable if I had offered to "take the problem off their hands." It would also have been setting up me, them, and the residential program for failure.

What was needed was a new way of thinking about their situation and the residential treatment, and we proceeded to build a theme for this admission based on some evidence that they and their son managed to get on well on some occasions. This was not a matter of my "selling" them the idea that they would solve the problem themselves. Once we focused on the times that *were* successful, rather than on the times that demonstrated the problem, they began to be able to approach the residential admission more optimistically.

The precise nature of this particular theme is not important here. What is important is recognizing that a new theme (or reframe of the placement) and setting of goals are not sufficient in themselves. We need constantly to highlight the idea that the residential process is one of transition or practice. The expectation of the families with whom we deal should be that there will be much hard work to do, back at home, after the placement has ended. Of course, if the view of their situation with which they came persists, then the idea that the problem may not be solved will be more evidence of failure. It is only after the establishment of a theme, which reframes the situation, builds on their existing strengths, and allows them to see the future differently, that the idea of "keeping on practicing at home" will be meaningful.

The "rites of passage" analogy is a helpful reminder of what our aims for the residential placement should be. The essence of the process is that it is one in which a change in status, with a change in the way people view themselves, is achieved. The reality is that various problems will persist, for that is part of life. Our hope is that a new view of self will lead people to feel more confident in handling these difficulties.

One of the underlying principles of my work is that my clients are the best judges of what is most helpful for them. I and a colleague have suggested that even young people who have been sexually abused are in the best position to decide what will be most helpful in therapy (Durrant & Kowalski, 1990). The same is true in the residential situation. If our focus is on achieving the outcome that we, as professionals, decide, then the process will inevitably be judged by that goal and clients will feel a pressure to succeed. If the emphasis is on our clients setting goals in the light of their experience, with a theme that flows from that, then it is easier to frame the process as one of practice in which everything that happens can serve the end of clients feeling their own control and competence.

Accordingly, a focus on practicing new skills and behaviors for the "real work" that lies ahead will involve our highlighting our clients' expertise, competence, and success at every point.

Returning to the example of Jeffrey from Chapter 4, a theme of "practicing having more good days" had been established. This theme seemed to make sense to Jeffrey and his mother. However, we ought not expect that ideas that have persisted for some time will magically be changed after only one interview. The therapist was concerned to finish the interview in such a way as to set the scene for what would follow. He wanted to highlight both the practice nature of the admission and the role Jeffrey and mother would be able to take in decision-making about the treatment.

Therapist: The idea the staff have at the moment is that on those days that you think are going to be "good days," they will allow you to make more decisions about what you do around here.

Worker: Do you think you will be able to tell us? Like if you want to make your own decisions and we are getting in your way.

Therapist: My guess is that you guys will need to practice. And you'll need to figure out what you think will be most helpful. Because my guess is that you know best what will help you figure out how to give yourself more good days. I figure that the staff here have lots of experience in working with kids, but they've never worked with you before. So you will be the person who knows best what will help you. Do you think you will be able to think about that?

Jeffrey: Yes.

Therapist: And you guys might need to practice. Some days you might feel like "I know I can do it. I know I can give myself a good day and keep myself out of trouble." Other days, you might feel like "No, I'm not feeling strong enough today. I need you to keep me out of trouble." And that's okay, that's part of practice. Like, when you practice shooting basketball, I guess some days you really feel like you'll get each one in, and other days you keep missing. Is that what happens?

Jeffrey: Yes.

Therapist: So it's the same with practicing having more good days. Some days you might feel like you can really do it, and other days it might seem like it's too hard. And that's okay. You might learn some things from the days that seem hard. And you will be the best judge of that.

The therapist hoped that Jeffrey and his mother had experienced this interview as a little different from some previous therapy experiences. It was likely that they were well used to therapy sessions that focused on what had been going wrong, and the focus of this interview on Jeffrey's strengths and mother's competence may have been different in itself. In seeking to ensure that this interview flowed "naturally" on to the practical aspects of the residential program, the therapist sought to reinforce Jeffrey's expertise in knowing what would be most helpful for him and to introduce the idea that a time of practice allows for mistakes as well as progress.

MARKING THE "NEW START"

In rites of passage, there is a separation or "leaving behind" of the past. We want to "mark" the admission to the program as a step in leaving the past behind. The interview or discussion in which the theme has been developed is an important part of this process, yet it is insufficient in itself. It is quite possible for the practical aspects of the admission to overshadow or work against the new ideas implicit in the theme.

In some programs, residents are allowed a "settling in" period before therapeutic work commences. Such a period is often seen as a "period of observation" in which staff make their assessments of the young person. To the child or adolescent, such a period may well be one in which he or she is acutely aware of having been "left behind in this place," and feelings of abandonment or of having been identified as the problem may quickly obscure new ideas contained in the interview theme. If the young person has experienced previous residential placements, this will be even more the case. Inevitably, the young person's response to this unsettling time will produce "disturbed" or "disturbing" behavior, which will be integrated into the assessment and leave everyone feeling even more daunted by the problems to be overcome.

Signing consent forms, listening to a reading of the "rules of the program," even being shown the physical layout of the premises can foster feelings in both the resident and his or her parents that they are entering a world in which they have no control (and, therefore, no value or competence).

Rather than standing back and observing, staff ought to use the time of entry into the program to highlight further the new framework. This can be achieved in small ways. Most programs have a set of rules or expectations for residents, and have them for good reason. These can be introduced in such a way that conveys the message, "You *must* comply with these," which can easily feel overwhelming. Alternatively, they can be discussed in a way that fits with the particular theme of this resident. This might be as simple as saying, "You have said that coming here is a chance for you to practice giving yourself more good days. Because we have a number of people here, we need some rules or guidelines about what kinds of things are okay. Let's go through these and you can tell us if you think these are the kinds of things that will help you have more good days." The discussion might also include questions such as, "Do you think you will be able to follow this rule? How come? Have you been able to do this in the past?"

In thinking of rules, I often suspect that many programs have more rules than are really necessary. However they are framed, rules still appear as criteria for external control. I have suggested that the basic thing with which we are dealing is the particular *experience* of this child or adolescent and his or her family. A daunting list of rules may work against our ability to take into account the particular way in which this young person makes sense of the situation. My preference is for a smaller set of rules, with other standards of acceptable and unacceptable behavior being related to the particular person. This is not an excuse for an "anything goes" regime. In Chapter 8, I outline a number of ways in which discipline may be approached, and unacceptable behavior dealt with, that fit with particular themes rather than appearing to be the imposition of arbitrary, external criteria.

There are other ways that the actual admission can be handled so as to complement the theme-setting process. Some programs use a "ritual" to mark the entry into the program and to frame it differently. This might be simply a matter of inviting the new resident and his or her parents to dinner in the residential unit on the first night and formally welcoming them. Such a welcome would involve restating the theme, for example, "This is Jeffrey, who is spending some time here practicing giving himself more good days, and his mother, who has been practicing letting Jeffrey figure out how to keep himself out of trouble and wants to keep practicing this." In a program where themes are commonplace, other residents might be introduced to the new resident and given an opportunity to reiterate their particular themes as well as mention the successes they have been having.

PRACTICING . . . OR REACHING HIGHER LEVELS?

Seeing the placement as a period of experimenting or of practicing new behaviors and forms of relationships has implications not only for how we respond to clients but also for the way the program is structured.

Some programs, often employing ideas from behavior theory, operate on a system of "levels." In such a system, residents begin their placement on a particular level and achieve "promotion" to successively higher levels as their behavior improves. The task of the placement becomes one of moving from "level 1" to "level 2," then behaving well enough to gain promotion to "level 3," and so on. Often, discharge from the program is earned by achieving the highest level, which may be called "graduation stage" or "discharge level." In some manifestations of this approach, infractions of acceptable behavioral standards may lead to demotion to a lower level.

Implicit in such a framework seems to be the assumption that change will occur as a progressive improvement. This assumption may be incompatible with ideas about transition and practice, since these are based more on assumptions that change is an "up and down" activity. My concern about "levels" systems is that, even though they appear to be based on rewarding successful behavior, they may easily contribute to ideas of failure. If the young people with whom we work have histories of problems and failure, they often enter the program with fairly negative views of themselves. They have much experience of people applying external criteria of acceptability to their behavior. Facing a set of "hurdles" for promotion to higher levels may easily evoke responses of "What's the point? I won't be able to do it." Since the prospect of promotion inevitably implies that higher levels are "better," it is much harder for temporary failure to be framed as an important part of practice.

> *Robert, aged 16 years, had been in the residential unit for four months. Referred from an acute psychiatric hospital, with a diagnosis of "bi-polar" disorder, he had a history of repeated placements, which were usually terminated when staff were unable to manage his uncooperative and sometimes destructive behavior. According to the staff of the unit, Robert came in "very oppositional and resistant. Initially, he didn't want to be here, didn't have a problem, but since then has turned that around."*
>
> *Robert is seen to have been doing well and believes that he is ready for discharge; however, he has not yet been promoted to "graduation level." Staff acknowledged that Robert was behaving well but were concerned his change may be superficial, with "no internalization." They were concerned about the expectations Robert had of himself and what his mother was going to expect of him, fearing that both Robert and his mother were being unrealistic about the future. This interview occurred shortly before his expected discharge.**

Therapist: Can you fill me in on how come you came here? I know it all seems like ancient history now, but it might be helpful for me to know.

Robert: Well, stealing cars was really it. And other stealing. And I started off at a group home. Then I vandalized the group home, and they put me in another group home. Then I ran from that group home, stole a car, and they put me in the hospital. Got out of there and went back to the group home for a month. Then I went back to the hospital for three months, then I came here. I didn't complete the program at the group home, and they had to find another place for me.

Therapist: So you've probably been in more of these places than I have.

---

*The therapist was Michael Durrant, with Kate Kowalski and Dr. Dana Christensen acting as a "team" for this consultation interview.

Robert: Yes.

Therapist: And it sounds like, in those other places, you were not very cooperative.

Robert: No, I wasn't.

Therapist: So that's four months and three days ago. Are things different now?

Robert: Pretty much.

Therapist: What were you like when you first came in here? Were you pleased to be here?

Robert: No, I was mad. I didn't want to be here, and it was hard. Then things started getting better.

Therapist: *(to Mother)* Do you think things are different now to when Robert first came in here?

Mother: Yes. I see him going back to before the trouble. Because before the trouble, he was a good boy. He was particular, concerned about my well-being and other people in the family. But at the end of the life of crime, he didn't care about anything or anybody. Now, the good boy's coming back. I think if he didn't get back to that, I think by now he'd be in a prison. And he's not mad at me any more.

Therapist: That's interesting. So you're clear that, before this trouble, he was a good boy. Things were going okay. And now, it was like this was an interruption in that, and things are getting back to how they were.

Mother: Yeah. He's still got a bit of an attitude, but it's not as bad as it used to be. He's pretty good.

Therapist: So, Robert, how have you managed to do this?

Robert: Figuring out that getting in trouble wasn't working any more, unless you want to stay locked up the rest of your life. The staff here helped me make up my mind.

Robert had found a job in a store, where it appeared he was a valued employee. The therapist was interested in exploring how he had managed to get the job, what things about him had impressed the manager who interviewed him. This was an effort to take advantage of the difference between "a boy who steals" and "a boy who is a trusted employee." Robert seemed to take this for granted, saying such things as, "It was on my treatment plan. It was required when I reached a certain phase that I go out and get a job." It was not clear if this represented that he saw himself as more in control and more responsible and so viewed the job as a logical development, or if it reflected that he was not taking credit for his own part in the achievement. The therapist was concerned that Robert saw getting a job as simply part of progressing to the next level rather than as a success that could be appreciated.

Mother saw the job as a sign that Robert was "back on track" and would be able again to be part of the family.

Therapist: Do you think he's started to care again?

Mother: I think so.

Therapist: So, Robert, what do you think you've learned about you from all this?

Robert: Well, I've learned that the things I was doing were wrong.

Therapist: But all this stuff, getting a job and doing well here. What does that tell you about the sort of guy you are?

Robert: I've got too much to lose. If I get locked up again, I'll lose everything and have to start all over. I don't want to do that.

Therapist: I've met some guys who don't care.

Robert: Well, those guys who don't care, they keep getting locked up time after time. I think I've had enough. I've been waiting to get out of this since last year.

Therapist: *(to Mother)* What if he comes back and . . . I guess like all kids, he's not going to do what he's told all the time.

Mother: Well, no, I expect that. And it seems like he grew up so fast. And I know he's not going to go and do everything I say and break his neck to do it.

Therapist: *(to Robert)* What makes you think Mum ought to trust you?

Robert: 'Cos I know what's right now.

Therapist: And you're pretty sure that you can be trusted? How do you think you'll do that?

Robert: Stay out of trouble.

Therapist: I guess it's easy to say that while you're here. How hard do you think it will be when you actually face it?

Robert: It depends how hard I want to do it. I think, when I go home, I'll be by myself for a while. Stay away from my friends.

Therapist: But staying out of trouble, and doing what your Mum tells you, and staying away from your friends — that will be pretty hard won't it?

Robert: It will be hard. Very hard. But I don't want to come back to a place like this.

Therapist: I need to shake your hand. I was starting to get worried that you were saying, "Hey, this will be real easy," but it sounds like you are being real sensible about it. I was glad when you said, "Yeah, it's going to be hard, but it's better than coming back to a place like this." So I was really glad. It made me think "Robert has really thought about this." But, at the same time, you're pretty sure you can do it?

Robert: I'm going to do it.

Therapist: *(to Mother)* What do you think will be the things that will tell you that you can trust him?

Mother: When he tells me he's one place, and he's at that place and not somewhere else. We did this over the weekend. I just want to know where he is and that he's going to be there. And I don't think that's asking too much.

Therapist: So you've been practicing that a bit?

Mother: Yes.

Therapist: So you've been practicing trusting him, and you've been practicing keeping yourself out of trouble.

Mother: He went across the street to watch a movie and I said, "Be home at 11." Well, he called at five after 11 and said, "The movie's not over yet, can I stay until it's over?" I said, "Sure," just 'cos he called. Now, if he hadn't called, I would go look for him.

Therapist: *(to Robert)* What would you have done a year or so ago?

Robert: I wouldn't have come home.

Therapist: You wouldn't have come home? You probably wouldn't even have been across the road, would you?

Robert: No.

Therapist: So you were able to take notice of what your Mum said. And even though you were having fun, you were able to concentrate on what your Mum said?

Robert: Yes.

Therapist: And before you said it was hard to keep yourself under control when you were with friends.

Robert: Yes, like sometimes I used to tell her I was going to a friend's house but I was out getting in trouble, and then two or three hours later I'd be in jail.

Therapist: So you guys have been practicing. Robert, you've been practicing staying out of trouble, and you've been practicing trusting him to keep himself out of trouble. And I guess, just like we said, it's going to be hard for Robert, so it will be hard for you to learn how to trust him. I guess one of the things that's hard for parents is that it's easy for you to get caught up in feeling that you've got to keep him out of trouble. But, Robert, you've said that you've figured out some ways for keeping yourself out of trouble.

The therapist was impressed that they had been using times of week-end leave to "practice" doing things differently. Mother's schedule had precluded frequent family sessions; however, she had received enough feedback about Robert's progress and received it in a way that had allowed her to use the period as one of practicing or experimenting as well. This was a good sign that she was not expecting everything to be "cured" by the time Robert returned home.

Both Mother and Robert seemed certain that he was ready to take the next step and return home. They were being fairly realistic, not seeing him as "cured" but acknowledging that there would be further difficulties and that it would take further practice to apply at home the things learned during the program. Staff also seemed to think Robert was ready to move on.

Unfortunately, Robert was on the level immediately below "discharge level" and so could not yet return home. Convinced that he was ready to go home, he became angry at this impediment, and his behavior deteriorated—hence he was demoted to the next lower level.

This is a good example of my concerns about such systems of "levels." If we are concerned about Robert's view of himself, it is clear that he is seeing himself as competent and ready to move on. Similarly, his mother seems to be viewing herself and their interaction in more optimistic terms. My contention is that it is this "view of self" that will be the major contributor to ongoing success, and his and his mother's view that he is ready to return home is most likely to lead to his being successful. The levels framework actively works against these emerging views of competence. In fact, the day-to-day "reality" of levels may mean that promotion to a higher level becomes a goal in itself rather than part of a more successful future. Moreover, since the levels and the standards required for promotion are external, the framework does not allow Robert or his mother to experience themselves as having any real control over their own achievement. Not only does the framework highlight failure, it also has the risk that success will be attributed to the framework rather than to individual achievement. This is suggested by the way in which Robert seems to attribute his success at gaining a job to the demands of the program rather than to his own efforts.

A system of levels depends upon standardized criteria for promotion. As such, it cannot take into account the individual meaning and experience of particular residents. In Chapter 8, I will suggest that discipline must take into consideration the particular experience of the child or adolescent involved and cannot simply reflect the imposition of external standards. "Rules" about promotion and demotion make this a much more difficult task. In addition, it is clear that the residential placement has been a time for both Robert and his mother to practice different behaviors. In discussing the establishment of a theme for placement, I have suggested that we can frame the situation in a way that makes sense both to the young person and to his or her parents as they think about the new skills, behaviors, and relationships that need to be practiced. Robert's case shows that the system of levels inevitably focuses on the resident's behavior and does not easily provide a way for including parents in the process as anything more than patient observers.

I would go so far as to suggest that the sole advantage of systems such as "levels" is that they appear to make life easier for staff, since they can treat every resident in the same way (although, we must acknowledge that, in the difficult task of residential treatment, making things easier for staff is an important and legitimate consideration and must remain an ongoing concern of the management of residential programs). However, the experience of every young person and family is different, and the way we respond to behavior must acknowledge this. What constitutes success that is meaningful to the particular resident cannot be codified but will be affected by the context. With a system of levels, achieving the highest level may overshadow everything else and so obscure the incremental nature of change and the ability to respond meaningfully to small steps along the way.

CONTRACTS—PROMISING TO GET BETTER?

I have similar concerns about the use of contracts in therapy and residential treatment. Many young people enter the residential program with a view of self that expects failure. Requiring that they agree to a contract may highlight their thoughts about the overwhelming nature of the task they face. It can almost seem as though we are asking them to promise to "get better" before they have been able to experience themselves in such a way as to make this a real possibility.

The previous chapter suggested that themes should be "goal directed."

Focusing on what things will be like when they are better allows us to be working *towards* something positive rather than simply moving *away* from some problem. However, contracts easily reify the goal state and may contribute to it seeming unattainable.

I have heard residential staff talk of a particular young person not being "really committed" to changing. Often this has been stated in terms of the resident not abiding by his or her contract. Despite our best intentions, the contract sometimes becomes the constant reminder of what has not yet been achieved.

If a young person was really able to sign a contract at the outset of a placement, committing himself or herself to particular changes or behaviors, it would require him or her to have a view of self as being able to achieve this. If he or she had such a view of self, a residential placement would probably be unnecessary!

Having said all this, it *may* be possible to use levels or contracts in different ways. If this is possible, it would require at the very least that the demands of the levels or the contract take into consideration the overall context of this young person's experience.

Making Practice Meaningful

In contrast to the implicit messages that may be contained in notions of levels or contracts, a program may embrace the idea of the placement as a period of practice, with the expectation that the person concerned will contribute to deciding the criteria for such practice and that both success and failure can be important parts of moving forward. This has implications not only for what we might do in therapy sessions, or how we respond to particular behaviors, but for how we frame all the day-to-day aspects of the program.

As part of the residential treatment, our clients leave for brief periods on passes. Rather than referring to the trip outside the facility as "being on a leave pass," we generally refer to this as "a practice excursion." We ask our residents to fill out a "practice excursion ticket"—a form that asks them to decide what it is they will practice while they are out and asks them to nominate the things they think they will notice themselves doing differently during this time. Staff will encourage residents to think about ways that they can use these practice excursions to demonstrate to themselves and to their families that they are making changes, and encourage them to set clear (and limited) expectations for themselves. We highlight the distinction between their experience of practic-

*ing new behaviors within the supportive environment of the facility
and the greater challenge of testing oneself in the "real world" during a
practice excursion.*

— *Prince William County Mental Health Services
Crisis/Detox Program, Manassas, Virginia*

Leave passes are often earned as rewards for good behavior. In this
program, however, they are part of the process of practice. If change is
going to occur outside rather than just in the program, periods of leave
are important aspects of this. Implicit in the way they are framed is the
idea that things may not go so well "out there" but that this is okay—it is
part of practice.

This is an example of only one part of a program, yet it demonstrates
the difference that thinking about practice might make. At any particular
time, both successes and failures may be framed and responded to in
terms of this time of practice, and so both may contribute to working
towards the goal.

The theme provides a way of thinking about and talking about the
process of the residential admission. It is anchored in the particular views
and experiences of the particular young person and family and provides a
coherent framework for experiencing the residential placement as a transition period. If we seek to focus on this experience, it is true that many
aspects of the program and of the role of staff are less predictable and less
structured than we might like. The following chapters attempt to provide
guidelines and examples for the process of responding to successful behavior and to unacceptable behavior in ways that make sense.

7

WATCHING the GRASS GROW: FOCUSING on SMALL STEPS and SUCCESSES

The period of "transition" that is the residential placement will be marked by ups and downs. With most adolescents in such a program, things do not always go smoothly, and so the day-to-day incidents provide the basic raw material for the treatment. The most effective programs will use these day-to-day events as part of the treatment process, since they are more immediate and more "real" than those things that might occur in more formal therapy sessions.

The question then becomes one of how best to respond to the things that occur. The young people with whom we are working will be well used to having people focus on the things they do wrong. A different focus may make an important difference in the way they experience the program.

LOOKING FOR EXCEPTIONS TO PROBLEM BEHAVIOR

Solution-focused brief therapy is a model or theory of therapy that rests on very different assumptions to those that underlie many more traditional approaches. In many ways, the basic ideas or assumptions of the solution-focused approach are very similar to the underlying principles I outlined in Chapters 1 and 2, which were suggested as ways of thinking about families who enter the residential treatment arena.

Developed by de Shazer and his colleagues (de Shazer, 1988, 1991, etc.), the approach begins from the point of view that it is better to focus on solutions rather than on problems. Problems are what get people stuck, and focusing on these may just lead to more stuckness. Solutions are the changes that people strive for, and focusing on these allows us to be more forward looking. This focus on solutions reflected the assumption (from Milton Erickson) that people already have a wealth of resources and strengths and that these are of more interest and more use than ideas about pathology and deficit.

I have discussed different ways of framing placements and establishing themes for a young person's time in the program. These are intended to give us a theme or way of organizing our thinking and responses around a common goal of helping young people (and families, if involved) experience themselves as competent and successful. Our hope is that they will leave the program seeing themselves as capable of living and relating successfully. Given that solution-focused therapy is an approach that focuses explicitly on such success, it provides a useful way of thinking about how to manage the day-to-day residential program.

We can learn from our mistakes (and the next chapter discusses how we may respond to such mistakes—problem behaviors—in ways that help residents experience themselves differently); however, we may learn even more from those things we are doing well. It is much easier to think about building on what's going right than it is to think about correcting or changing what's going wrong.

The main role of residential staff is to be on the lookout for and respond to any small signs of success or solution behavior. This may seem a bit like "watching the grass grow," since it sometimes involves looking for extremely small signs and responding to incremental progress.

> Anita had been in the residential program for four weeks, although she had absconded frequently and had been absent more than she had been present. One Friday evening, as the dinner plates were cleared away, a staff member brought out a colorfully-iced cake and set it on the table. The children's expressions showed some surprise—cakes were not common residential food, and they were unaware that it was anybody's birthday. The residential staff member moved the cake in front of Anita and invited her to cut it. She did this with a look of confusion on her face. Finally, the staff member said, "Anita has managed to stay here for six days in a row. That's the longest she has been able to stay here, and we thought it deserved a cake."
>
> —Alternatives for Families, Inc., Kenora, Ontario

Anita's persistent running away was frustrating and staff were aware of the possibility that they could become caught in a spiral of unsuccessful attempts to deal with it. Their assumption was that Anita's view of herself led to her not feeling able to resist running away, and her absences often followed some altercation or other problem. They realized that they and Anita (and the other children) had become focused on her absences, and that this simply added to everyone's frustration. The fact that Anita had stayed for six days was something different, something successful, although it was likely that no one had taken much notice of it. This simple way of highlighting this evidence of success was a way of reorienting everyone's focus towards Anita's ability to keep herself in the program (successful behavior that might be built upon) rather than towards her inability to do so (problem behavior that does not give people much hope). The slight sense of mystery that they were able to introduce by making the most of people's surprise at the appearance of the cake probably helped make the event more meaningful.

In discussing this incident later, a staff member commented that she knew why Anita had not run away this particular week—there was a fishing excursion planned for the weekend, and Anita knew that she would be prevented from going if she had run away. It would have been easy for staff to dismiss her success by thinking, "She only stayed because she wanted something!" However, their view was that the reason she had stayed was less important than the fact that she had done so. Her success warranted acknowledgment, whatever the reason might have been, for acknowledging this success might allow Anita to see herself differently (or, at least, to experience other people reacting to her differently) and so might offer some hope for the future.

Similarly, it would be easy for staff to focus on her continued running away rather than on her (perhaps temporary) staying, and so to have the view that presenting a cake in this situation was just "reinforcing her bad behavior." However, they had already tried various punishments and consequences, and these had been unsuccessful. To continue on this tack would have increased their frustration and perhaps led them to the view that Anita was seeking to sabotage her treatment. It would also have been likely to lead Anita to think, "What's the point?" and to feel more out of control. Their response, by trying to build upon what was different about this incident, left everyone with the possibility of feeling optimistic. If Anita was able to appreciate the fact that she had shown some control by staying six days, then there might be the possibility of her seeing herself as being able to stay seven, or eight, or ten days. She might even respond to her success being highlighted by giving up running away.

This is a good example of the fact that the important thing is how we *think* about the behavior of the adolescents and children in our programs.

If we honestly believe that they are capable of successful behavior we will be more likely to be able to notice such events and respond to them.

The essential notion of exceptions is that, no matter how pervasive the problem may seem, *nothing happens all the time.* If people can "notice" those times things happen differently – more successfully – then they have something that might be built upon.

> Problems are seen to maintain themselves simply because they maintain themselves and because clients depict problems as *always happening.* Therefore, times when the complaint is absent are dismissed as trivial by the client or even remain completely unseen, hidden from the client's view. Nothing is actually hidden, but although these exceptions are open to view, they are not seen by the client as differences that make a difference. For the client, the problem is seen as primary (and the exceptions, if seen at all, are seen as secondary), while for therapists the exceptions are seen as primary; interventions are meant to help clients make a similar inversion, which will lead to the development of a solution. (de Shazer, 1991, p. 58)

Exceptions are important because they are things that the client is already doing rather than things imposed by a therapist. By and large, most people find it easier to build on something they are already doing than to start out something new – we just have to help young people and parents recognize that they are already doing these things. de Shazer sees the focus on exceptions as fitting with Milton Erickson's idea of utilization, and defines it as "Utilizing whatever the client does that is somehow 'right,' 'useful,' 'effective,' 'good' or 'fun' for the purposes of developing a solution" (de Shazer, 1988, p. 140). To this list, we might add whatever the client does that is "different."

Within the residential program, this means staff looking for any examples – no matter how small and seemingly insignificant – of successful, competent, or nonproblem behavior and drawing attention to them.

This can be quite a test of how staff think about things. For example, an adolescent with a history of violent assaults upon people may have an outburst in the residential unit one day and break a number of windows. This behavior may need to be dealt with in some way (and this is discussed in the next chapter); however, the fact that the adolescent broke windows on this occasion rather than breaking other people's heads may be an important exception that can be highlighted. Of course, it may not be appropriate to mention this at the time of the breaking glass, but it is something that may usefully be discussed later when things have settled down. This requires staff, even in the midst of difficult or crisis situations, to think in terms of looking for such exceptions. For a young person who has experienced himself as out-of-control, the fact that someone notices that his violence on this occasion was directed at property rather than people (and so can be seen to represent some progress) may be a powerful beginning to thinking differently about himself. Such a different focus can often provide a way to move forward with the adolescent, rather than adolescent and staff becoming increasingly involved in an escalating pattern, which may lead to the young person being asked to leave the program.

Looking for exceptions is more than just "highlighting the positives." While doing this is important, there is a risk of this becoming a formula technique applied unthinkingly — and techniques applied in this way tend not to work. This approach to residential treatment is about *meaning*, and everything must be judged according to how it contributes to the young person building a different way of thinking about him or herself. "Reinforcing positive behavior" is an idea from learning theory, and "the power of positive thinking" is a popular idea in many circles; however, a "solution focus" is more than either of these. It may seem repetitive to say that it involves the overall "stance" we take — the assumptions we have as we approach our therapeutic task — but this is a crucial point that bears repetition. It is quite possible to highlight positive behavior in such a way as to fail to make a difference. If it is simply a technique, clients will see through it very quickly. If we reinforce positive behavior without taking into account how the child or adolescent may make sense of our response, it will fail to make a difference and may actually make worse a sense of hopelessness. I have had a number of cases where I highlighted exceptions to my clients and found that their reaction was something like, "Yes, I managed it then, so it makes me feel even more of a failure when I can't do it."

In the example of the violent adolescent, a staff member (preferably one whom the adolescent knows and trusts) might take him aside the following day and say, "Hey, I heard about yesterday. It sounds like you got pretty mad, and I hear that you ended up smashing six windows. That was some tantrum! John told me that he's going to speak to you about helping get the windows fixed, but the other thing he told me was that you only smashed windows, you didn't smash anybody's head. How were you able to do that?" It is likely that the adolescent will not be able to answer this, since he may not have experienced himself as having control over his anger at the time. "I remember hearing about how you used to smash people's heads in when you got angry, and we've seen things like that happen around here, so I'm really interested that you did it differently yesterday. Even when you were so angry, how come you were able to keep a bit of self-control?"

The adolescent is probably not used to thinking about his outbursts in terms of *having* some control, so is likely still to be unable to answer such questions. That is okay, and it is not helpful to keep haranguing him until he answers. Rather, the very fact of these questions may encourage him to begin to think differently.

The discussion might continue with, "Can you think of the last time you showed some self-control like that? Maybe not a time you were quite that angry, but a time when you could have lost control and managed to keep it?" Or, "So, if you are able to build on this control a bit, how do you think it will make a difference around here?" Such questioning may continue at the time, or be resumed casually at a later time; in any event, the aim is to encourage the adolescent to begin to think about himself and his anger differently.

The adolescent may "explain away" his apparent episode of self-control. "Well, there was no one around to hit, so I had to smash the windows." Or, "I don't know, I wasn't thinking about what I was doing." It is important not to try to convince him that he actually showed self-control. We can remain puzzled about how come this time was different, and leave the idea to percolate. This one incident of an exception being noticed may not make a huge difference, but a climate in which staff are attuned to noticing such examples, or framing behavior as successful, may have a powerful effect over time.

The important thing here is not whether the particular behavior **was** an example of greater competence or success, but whether it can be **framed,** or highlighted, as such and so be given a more positive meaning. Any small steps can be highlighted like this, although they must be plausible enough to lead to some thought.

> *Jason, age 14, had persistently seemed unable to accept responsibility for his behavior. He attributed his running away and risk-taking behavior to his father's girlfriend, whom he did not like; he attributed his earning money by prostitution to his father's unwillingness to give him the money he needed for drugs; and he saw his drug and alcohol use as a response to the hassles he had to cope with. His father had been working harder and harder to keep Jason out of trouble. One way of seeing their situation was that they had become caught in an escalating pattern of Jason taking less responsibility for himself and Dad taking more. Jason's residential admission was framed as a time of practice for Jason to feel that he could take responsibility for his own life, and a*

time for Dad to practice behaving in a way that invited Jason to assume such responsibility.

Within the residential unit, the pattern was equally clear. On one occasion, when he was found smoking marijuana, he claimed that he needed it because it helped him get on with other people. He would often come to staff and complain about other residents, demanding that staff take some action about the small things the other residents were doing to annoy him. Staff would sometimes comment to him that it was easy to fall into the pattern of trying to make the drugs responsible or make the staff responsible, and tried to talk with him about how it might be different if he felt he could take this responsibility himself.

After a while, Jason went through a period of getting into fights with other residents who upset or annoyed him. Staff members initially tried to deal with these incidents through punishment, or by talking with him about how to resolve his differences in a nonviolent way, but this was not very successful. After discussion amongst themselves, staff came to the conclusion that their responses were simply feeding in to the established pattern, since they were trying to take responsibility for Jason's behavior changing. At the same time, they could not just stand by as he attacked other residents.

Thinking about how to frame Jason's behavior differently, they realized that Jason was actually attempting to sort out his difficulties with other residents himself. While his attempts were clearly inappropriate, this was still different from his previous pattern of complaining to staff and expecting them to do something about the situation. One of the staff talked to Jason and commented that the staff had just realized that Jason was taking responsibility himself for his disagreements with the other kids. "You know that fighting is not on, and so we've got a bit caught up in the fact that you have been fighting, and we didn't realize that this was actually a way you were trying to take responsibility yourself for sorting these things out. That's a pretty big change from when you kept asking us to sort it out for you." There was some discussion about how this was different, with the youth worker wondering what had made Jason decide he was ready to try to take such responsibility himself (which, of course, he didn't know—all he could think of was that the other kids were annoying him so he had to do something about it). Then, after acknowledging that taking this responsibility was new for Jason, the worker wondered if Jason would like some help in figuring out how to deal with these situations differently.

Previous attempts to "educate" Jason about handling conflict had not

*worked, since they too easily sounded like efforts to have him acknowl-
edge that his behavior was wrong, and since they contributed to the
responsibility pattern that had been pervasive. Framing this new behavior as an exception to the previous pattern placed it in a different light.
Behavior that was previously seen as negative was now framed as the
first few steps of doing something different, and so suggested something different about Jason. The staff were then in a position to work
with Jason to help him "refine" his new behavior rather than seeking to
modify it, and he was able to respond to these suggestions.*

—Robinson House, Care Force Youth Services, Sydney

Different Ways of Highlighting Exceptions and Successes

I well remember a young man in a residential unit who had managed
some different, more positive behavior (I don't remember what it was, but
that is not important here). One staff member had commented on the
behavior and, as another walked into the room, the young man said, "I
suppose you are going to tell me that you're very impressed!" He had
become used to staff highlighting exceptional behavior and so further
congratulatory comments didn't make a difference. (On the other hand,
this might show that *he* had acknowledged that his behavior was something that might bring such compliments, and so this was perhaps evidence that he was noticing such things about himself.)

Like parents, residential staff can become predictable, and predictable
behavior may be dismissed more easily. There are countless different ways
to respond to small successes, and staff are encouraged to explore as many
different ways as possible. Sometimes, a response will flow naturally from
the "theme" that has been constructed for the placement, sometimes it
will flow from the particular staff member's relationship with the resident,
and sometimes it will just be a matter of a small comment that is meaningful for the resident.

As with most aspects of the therapy and residential process, there are
no hard-and-fast rules about how to do it—although we can draw out some
ideas about what *not* to do.

Sometimes it can be appropriate and meaningful to congratulate the
resident on a particular example of different behavior; however "going
over the top" in congratulation is usually counterproductive as it runs the
risk of seeming false to the young person. Moreover, the message "that
was terrific" may evoke the response, "No, it wasn't really." If the young
person is caught up in seeing him or herself as incompetent, out-of-control,

or a failure, he or she is likely to interpret things in ways that fit with that view. A positive reaction from staff that is too discrepant from the young person's view and experience may lead to it being dismissed and may lead to the young person attributing the success to external factors rather than to different behavior on his or her own part. Of course, the congratulations of staff can be meaningful, and can help the resident feel good about a small step forward, but it is ultimately more important that the resident himself or herself see the behavior as successful rather than the staff doing so.

Similarly, staff and therapists can make the same error in reporting to parents about the resident's behavior. Being too enthusiastic in recounting a successful step, particularly a small one, may invite a "yes, but . . . " response, since it may seem too far removed from the parents' experiences of their son or daughter. Telling parents how wonderful their child is too easily allows them to feel that their experience of frustration and feelings of failure are being discounted. Inviting them to speculate on the success is more likely to lead to their beginning to see things differently.

In the same vein, trying to convince the resident or parents that something was an exception is not usually helpful. We need to believe in the power of difference. In the title of his recent book, de Shazer (1991) describes this as *Putting Difference to Work*. Difference can work for us, and we can leave it to do much of the work. If we can bring a piece of different behavior into prominence, highlight it by asking questions about it, then it will have some effect. Rather than our pronouncing the importance of an exception, it is often better to be curious about it. We can contrast it with previous behavior, ask how the person concerned makes sense of it, wonder about how he or she was able to do it, and speculate about what difference it might make. In this way, we invite the person concerned to think about the event and its meaning. Making a proclamation about success is easier and may feel better to us; however, leaving the young person and/or parents with questions that highlight the exception and its meaning may be more useful in the longer term. My colleague, Kate Kowalski, has referred to the "Colombo approach." Those familiar with the TV detective will recall his constant quizzical questions about what behavior or evidence might mean, which has the disarming effect of leaving people to figure it out for themselves.

The role of staff is to provide a framework that will make it more likely that exceptions will be noticed.

Jill, age 12, lived with her mother and brother, and her father lived in another state. Although the parents had legally divorced six years ago, the process of divorcing continued with ongoing tension and con-

flict. Jill had found herself living a life of sickness, sadness, and helplessness as she tried to deal with her future. As a result of this, Jill's mother was finding it more and more difficult to be around her, and a residential admission was sought.

We framed the situation as one in which the pressures and the feelings of hopelessness had got in the way of Jill's growing up. While she was at an age where she would normally be experimenting with being grown up, the events in her life had meant she had been growing down instead. We wanted to acknowledge the fact that external and family difficulties had seemed to trigger Jill's problems but wanted to do so in a way that might allow her to see herself as having some control or agency herself, to see the possibility of doing something different. The idea of "growing up or growing down" seemed to make sense to Jill (and her mother), and she said she was interested in exploring ways of growing up.

As part of the program, we asked Jill to build a dial in the shape of a half circle with the ends of the dial being "0" and "10" and with a pointer attached to mark her place on the dial. The area less than 5 was shaded and marked "growing down" and that over 5 was shaded and marked "growing up." A staff member talked with Jill and her mother about what kinds of things she would be doing for each area. It was important that we have her identify specific behaviors (so it was meaningful rather than vague) and that the indicators of growing up and of growing down be not just defined in terms of "socially acceptable" behaviors but in broader terms (how Jill would be feeling, what things people would notice about her, and so on). This list was posted on the unit under the dial.

Jill was asked to set the dial each morning according to the direction that she was to be working, and staff and Mom would then respond accordingly. We discussed that if she were working on growing down, then staff and Mom would need to be more attentive to her as she would need to be looked after more. If she were working on growing up, then Mom and staff would know to back off and allow her more room to accomplish tasks on her own. If what she was doing was inconsistent with her dial, according to her list, then we would ask for clarification.

In the past, it had been easy to see Jill's behavior globally and usually in terms of her difficulties. The dial, particularly the growing up side of it, encouraged Jill to plan and think about, and staff to notice and respond to, those things she did that were different. In this case, we included the "problem" behavior on the dial (the growing down end), since it helped draw a distinction with the behavior at the other end and also helped reinforce the idea that this was a time of practice when *things would not always go smoothly. What was important, however, was that growing down days would not be responded to punitively but with "increased attention" that fit with the frame. In addition, if Jill identified a day as a growing down day according to the dial, there were still exceptions to which staff could respond. One was the very fact that she could accurately predict or monitor behavior that was worth highlighting. Further, a growing down day alerted us to be aware of any (small) indications that Jill might be "turning around" her day and having a try at growing up practice.*

As she practiced growing up, the dial was an obvious and consistent reminder to her, her mother when she visited, and staff, as the pointer spent more and more time at the upper end of the dial. With this reminder, staff and Jill were "motivated" to be on the look out for any signs that might move the dial higher. Over time, Jill was able to find options to the sickness, sadness, and helplessness, and for her discharge celebration she was given a "key to the future" indicating she had control over which direction she would go.

—Shadow Mountain Institute, Tulsa, Oklahoma

In this case, the dial was a tangible way of indicating behavior. Since the pointer being at the upper end of the scale was the goal, the constant presence of the dial was an encouragement to look for grown-up behavior.

The various ways of highlighting exceptions and successes, so that the young person will notice and make sense of them, are limited only by the creativity of staff members (and, perhaps, as the next example suggests, by their willingness to appear "slightly crazy").

Cricket is a popular summer sport in Australia. As the batsman faces the bowler, he seeks to hit the ball and score runs. A hit that goes right to the boundary of the field automatically scores four runs, without the batsman having to run. A hit over the fence scores six runs, and "fours" and "sixes" are considered displays of great batting skill. It is the job of the umpire on the field to determine whether or not a ball has reached, or gone over, the fence, and the umpire uses various hand signals to indicate to the official scorers the fate of the shot. These hand signals are quite distinct and well-known to cricket devotees (for example, when a batsman hits a "six," which is the supreme humiliation of the bowler, the umpire raises both arms above his head).*

---

*The details of the game, and of these signals, will mean nothing to readers in noncricketing nations such as America. However, this is not important, and creative residential staff could probably use similar ideas utilizing aspects of baseball.

Tim, age 11, was in a residential unit following a long history of temper outbursts. In the initial stages of his placement, a theme had been constructed of Tim beating his temper rather than the temper beating him. Staff discovered that Tim was an enthusiastic cricket follower and began to talk with him about his temper bowling to him and trying to bowl him out. Gradually, they used various cricket terms as metaphors for Tim's struggle against his temper—talking about his temper bowling him out and him scoring runs by hitting his temper around the ground. *

It was sometimes quite disconcerting to visitors to the residential unit when, in the midst of some activity or conversation, a staff member would suddenly jump up and extend both arms in the air. Tim would look bemused, and other staff (and, sometimes, residents) would applaud or murmur their approval. To Tim, this was a sign that he had hit his temper for six—he had kept or regained control at a time when he might have been expected to lose his temper—and it was a novel and meaningful way to draw attention to an exception.

On occasion, staff would make some comment about the way that the temper had bowled to Tim and tried to trap him (such as when another resident had annoyed him or when he had not got his own way with some request) and wonder how Tim had been skillful enough to hit a scoring shot from this. On other occasions, staff might talk with Tim after a particular incident and ask him about how he had managed to keep such control. Sometimes, the very fact of the "six" being noticed and publicly signalled was sufficient. No one "kept score," although there were occasions when staff or other residents would remark on the number of scoring shots Tim had managed, and he seemed pleased at this.

— Timaru Hostel, Care Force Youth Services, Sydney

What is important about this example is that the ways of drawing attention to the exceptions were meaningful to Tim. Staff had noticed Tim's passion for cricket and had joked with him about it. Initially, this metaphor had been used in relation to Tim's temper problem as part of this joking. However, when staff noticed that Tim responded enthusiastically to their comments, they realized that this way of responding was one that fit for Tim. As such, the signals provided a kind of "short hand" way of responding that was meaningful to Tim. Also, drawing attention to these excep-

---

*For a detailed example of the use of such a sporting metaphor in highlighting a young man's victories against his problem, see Durrant (1985).

tions was probably as important in helping staff see Tim differently as in helping him notice his successes.

Noticing, and responding to, successes and exceptions is important in helping the client begin to see him or herself differently. However, residential staff have often reported that the process helps them build a different picture of the client as well, which then makes a difference in their responses.

Eleven-year-old Steve would not stay with the group during a day out to Blue Mountains. He continually disappeared, only to be found climbing outside the safety fence above a 2,000-foot drop. The staff member felt no control over Steve at all as every time he reprimanded him it had no effect. Trying to think of ways to control him, and conscious of the responsibility to ensure his safety, the youth worker tried explaining the situation to Steve, insisting that he remain by his side, and so on. Finally, in total frustration, he gave up.

In the residential unit, one aspect of Steve's program had been his regularly shading in on a chart how much in control of his feelings he thought he was. Instead of trying to think of some more draconian way of dealing with Steve's behavior on the outing, the youth worker found a piece of paper and had Steve draw a number of freehand shapes on it. "These shapes," he said, "are the different parts of today. One shape could be the time before we left this morning, one shape might be the time in the bus driving up here, another the time up until lunch, and so on. Can you tell me which shape is which part of the day?" Somewhat sullenly at first, Steve did this and was willing to shade in each shape according to how much he thought he had been in control of his feelings during that part of the day. The resulting shapes showed that Steve had started the day with quite a lot of control, had less control as the day went on, but had had times when his control was greater. Steve was happy to talk for a few minutes with the youth worker about how come he had had that much control at different times of the day, and his behavior was greatly improved for the remainder of the trip.

— Timaru Hostel, Care Force Youth Services, Sydney

In discussing this incident later, the youth worker commented that he was not sure whether this exercise primarily made a difference to Steve or whether its main effect was to help him, the youth worker, see Steve differently. As they had become embroiled, more and more, in a focus on Steve's lack of cooperation, they were led further into a "battle of wills," which left no possibility for either to experience success. The exercise provided a break from the problem, as they sat together and worked on the shapes, and encouraged both to begin to think in terms of how much control Steve did have. This changed the focus and allowed both Steve and the youth worker to see him as someone who exercises control over his feelings much of the time. This provided a much better foundation for mutual cooperation during the rest of the outing.

CREATING A CLIMATE THAT ENHANCES SUCCESS

The day-to-day residential program is one in which staff try to find as many opportunities, in as many ways as possible, to respond to even the smallest signs that residents are having success or are taking steps forward. From a theoretical point of view, this approach *assumes* that there will be many such examples of success, that there will be many exceptions to problem behavior. It is not a matter of creating exceptions. If we believe they are there, we will find them. However, they will not always be obvious, and residents or other staff will not always think them significant, so the manner in which we respond is important.

Cade and O'Hanlon (1993), in discussing different models of therapy, describe how therapists from different theoretical perspectives "discover" evidence for their own particular favored explanation. They point out how behavioral therapists "discover" behavioral problems, biologically oriented therapists "discover" chemical imbalances, systems therapists "discover" skewed hierarchies, and so on. Once we believe in something, we are more likely to discover evidence for its existence. Similarly, competency-based therapists or workers are more likely to "discover" examples of competence. As we believe that competency and exceptions exist, we will be more likely to find them and respond to them. As we do this, we help create a climate in which clients will be more likely to notice and respond to these aspects of their experience.

In discussing the therapy situation, de Shazer gives an example of beginning a second therapy session simply by asking, "What's better?" (1991, p. 144). Such an opening move clearly reflects the therapist's assumption that there will be something that is better and so the client simply has to choose which improvement to mention. On the other hand, had he asked, "How have things been?" that might imply that some things have been better and some worse, leaving the client to decide whether to mention success or failure. When the therapist begins from the position that there will have been some success, it is more likely that the client will be able to identify success. As the client identifies it, and discusses it, it becomes "real."

Similarly, residential staff who operate from the assumption that the young people in their care will show signs of progress will find these signs. The challenge then is one of how to respond to them so that the young person begins to build a different picture of success. This is similar to the way parents are alerted to their son or daughter's progress, which will be discussed in detail later.

How can residential staff create a "climate" that makes it most likely that exceptions will be noticed and highlighted? Here are a few suggestions:

- In writing up files or daily reports, staff could have some standard questions they use in helping them assemble their information. For example, "What evidence has there been today that this young person is improving/is taking small steps/is worth our sticking with?" "What are one or two examples of times today when the old behavior could have been shown but wasn't?" "What did this resident do today that was different or surprised us?"

- Regular staff meetings are often times when "problems" are shared, with the possible result that staff confirm each other's problem-focused view of particular residents. Instead, staff meeting agendas could commence with an item such as "What's been better this week?"—either in reference to the unit as a whole, or as part of discussing each resident.

- There may, of course, be particular difficulties that staff need to discuss and formulate ways of responding to. Often, it can be useful to ask one another, "How have we been seeing/responding to this? How could we see it differently? How could we respond differently?"

- Meal times and group meetings provide times when staff could deliberately try to mention exceptions they have noticed.

These are only some suggestions. Different ideas will fit for different programs. The important thing to remember is that most of us have been taught to look for problems. Looking for exceptions or successes does not always come naturally, and anything a group of staff can do to create a climate that encourages a focus on exceptions will help the residential unit focus on competence.

8

DISCIPLINE in the RESIDENTIAL UNIT: RESPONDING to DIFFICULT BEHAVIOR in a WAY THAT MAKES a DIFFERENCE

As I have pointed out earlier, the idea that the period of residential admission is a "trial and error" or practice period means that ups and downs are to be expected. If a young person has had a history of difficult behavior before coming into the residential unit, and he or she (and others around him or her) has become used to that behavior, it is clearly unrealistic to expect that things will begin to improve immediately after admission. Framing the placement as a period of practice helps create a climate that does not perpetuate feelings of failure by setting unrealistic expectations of immediate change, and allows for the fact that the process may not be smooth.

However, this does **not** mean that any and all behavior can be tolerated. The idea of a period of transition or practice does not mean that "anything goes." Out-of-control, disruptive, or unacceptable behavior may be expected but does not have to be accepted. The question for residential workers, as they grapple with issues of discipline and with managing difficult behavior in the day-to-day activities of the program, is how to deal with unacceptable behavior in a way that fits with the therapeutic focus of the rest of the program.

DISCIPLINE AS A MEANS FOR GIVING NEW INFORMATION

Everything we do during the course of the placement must be measured against the question "How does this contribute to the development of new experiences and a new view of self?" The framing of the placement, any individual program, and any specific therapy or counseling are easily seen as parts of this process and may be tailored towards this aim. It is less easy to see how the day-to-day interactions may be considered similarly, and "discipline" is an area where many struggle to find ways to be "therapeutic." However, discipline (or "punishments" or "consequences") are actions that occur at those very crucial moments when problematic behavior is happening. If we can find a way to respond to these events in a therapeutic manner, we can harness these naturally occurring and salient occasions as part of our overall process of treatment.

If an adolescent has a history of temper tantrums and out-of-control behavior, our aim during the placement is that he or she should be able to develop a view of him or herself as being capable of exercising control and not feeling overwhelmed by emotions and reactions that seem overpowering. We may frame the placement in a way that seeks to facilitate this and may include some specific counseling that addresses this issue. Inevitably, there will be occasions when the resident will display out-of-control behavior. How do we respond to such outbursts? We can either respond in a way that seeks, first and foremost, to modify or correct the misbehavior or we can respond in a way that seeks primarily to further the process of the adolescent seeing things (and self) differently. Exceptions to the problem behavior provide important foundations for developing this new view. However, the times at which the problem behavior actually occurs and the ways that staff respond are also ideal times to influence the way the adolescent thinks about the tantrums and about his or her own control.

In many areas of our lives, we learn from those times when things go wrong. Such times are relevant and immediate. We can practice, we can anticipate, we can plan how to do things differently, but all these endeavors (though useful) may seem somewhat abstract. The times we actually "mess up" are the times when the behavior and the possibility of alternatives may be most meaningful. However, these are also the times when feelings and memories about "old" meanings of failure or lack of control may be strongest.

Discipline is commonly thought of as a way to modify behavior. It is something that authority figures do to those who misbehave in order to ensure that the misbehavior does not happen again. That's the problem — if *you* do something to control *my* behavior, then it does not help me think of *myself* as able to exercise control. Residential staff taking control of residents' behavior is often easier and quicker, yet it may work against the things we are trying to achieve.

A colleague (Don Coles) suggested some time ago that we could helpfully think of discipline as a means for giving new information about self rather than as a way to modify behavior. This is an important distinction since it reflects what we think our intervention is all about. It may not mean that what we *do* in response to misbehavior is always different, but it will mean that the way we *think* about what we do will be different.

REACTING OR RESPONDING?

I remember a story from some years ago about a television interview with the captain of a jumbo jet, which had mysteriously "dropped" a few thousand feet during a flight.* Apparently, the crew had been able to correct the problem within about five seconds. Had they taken only a second or two longer, it would have been too late to get the plane back under control, and they would have plunged to certain disaster. The captain was asked, "What was the first thing you did when you realized what was happening?" His reply, to the confusion of the reporter, was, "The first thing I did was sit on my hands." Seeing her consternation, he explained, "If I hadn't, I might have reacted without thinking and made a real mess of the situation."

When children misbehave, parents tend to react. They try to deal with the situation in terms of appropriate punishment, and their reaction will be influenced by the misbehavior itself but also often by their general level of frustration with their child, their own state of mind, what else is going on in the house at the time, and so on. By and large, as a parent I find myself acting (or shouting) first and thinking later.

For many parents and children, parents' reactions work out okay because they happen within the context of a long-term relationship. For many of the children and adolescents in residential placements, however, their experience has been of parents' reactions that have escalated in severity or that have left them feeling hurt, humiliated, or more defiant.

*This story is reproduced here from memory. I saw the television interview, but was reminded of the story by my colleague, Gerard Menses, some years later while we were together in a plane!

Moreover, parenting is a developmental process rather than a therapeutic or specifically change-oriented activity. Residential treatment, on the other hand, is very much a therapeutic or change-oriented process. Residential staff, no matter how close they may get to some of the children or adolescents in their care, are not surrogate parents. They do not have the same history of relationship nor the same emotional ties, and their work with adolescents and children has a clear focus (in fact, my observation is that it is precisely when residential staff begin to see themselves as substitute parents that they find themselves becoming caught in feeling over-responsible, suffering burn-out, and beginning to react unthinkingly!).

The work of residential staff has a clear *purpose* and is therapeutic in its aim. Whether or not the program overtly involves therapy, all residential staff are concerned with helping residents make changes that will allow more successful lives. Thus, unlike parents, residential staff have a therapeutic focus. While parents react, the role of residential staff is to *respond*. Responding entails acting in ways that are consistent with the overall aim of the placement, and it involves thinking about what we do.

When a child or adolescent misbehaves, we may react to the behavior by expressing our displeasure and/or frustration, which is then demonstrated in some form of punishment, or we may respond in a way that deals with the misbehavior in a manner that furthers our overall therapeutic aim for the resident. It is important to see that no single piece of behavior happens in isolation. Our responses to misbehavior must be considered in the light of the whole process we are undertaking with the child or adolescent rather than as an immediate reaction to the particular incident. Sometimes, a consideration of the whole therapeutic process will require that we respond very differently from the way we would if we were simply considering how to deal with an isolated piece of behavior. In this way, the purpose of our work with young people means that our task, and our responses to behavior, are very different to those of parents, teachers, and other authority figures.

Our focus on competence and meaning, and the themes we might develop as a way of thinking about a particular placement, may provide ways of responding to unacceptable behavior that offer new information and alternatives. Molnar and Lindquist (1989) describe a number of ways that brief therapy ideas may be used to devise different ways of dealing with problem behavior in the school classroom situation. They offer numerous examples of ways that different responses — responses that focused on meaning rather than simply on control — allowed students and teachers to escape the escalating confrontations that otherwise tended to occur. We may adopt similar ideas in dealing with unacceptable behavior in the residential situation.

PUNISHMENT VS. CONSEQUENCES

Many people are familiar with the distinction between "punishment" and "consequences."

According to the Oxford Dictionary, *punish* means "to cause an offender to suffer for an offence . . . as retribution or requital, or as a caution against further transgression," and *punishment* is "that which is inflicted as a penalty." *Consequence* is "a thing or circumstance which follows as an effect or result from something preceding; . . . a logical result."

If a child refuses to turn off the TV when asked, and I say, "For that, you cannot have supper," that is a punishment. It is intended to cause the child to suffer and, presumably, to be a retribution and a warning not to do it again. If, on the other hand, I ask the child to turn off the TV and then go ahead and serve supper without him, so he watches TV and misses his meal, that is a consequence. I have not imposed the loss of the meal, I have simply not protected him from the logical result of not turning off the TV when asked.

Part of learning to be, and to see myself as being, responsible or having personal agency involves learning that my behavior has consequences. Although the unpleasantness of an arbitrary penalty or punishment may make me think twice before repeating the same behavior, it may not assist me towards a view of greater responsibility since it is something imposed or done to me by someone else. Experiencing the natural consequences of my behavior, however, may not only help me realize the (possibly) unpleasant effects but may allow me to see that I have some control over avoiding these by behaving differently. For anybody, the experience of having some personal agency or control over one's own behavior and its consequences is one of the key contributors to self-esteem and the development of a view of self as competent.

Therefore, it is usually better, wherever possible, to allow the natural consequences of misbehavior to prevail rather than concocting an arbitrary punishment. Simple and commonsense though this may sound, it is extremely easy for residential staff to find themselves preoccupied with punishment and ignoring natural consequences. This is often because natural consequences may not, at first, appear "severe enough." Having to help repair damaged property, for example, may not "feel" as severe as being given additional, unpleasant domestic tasks. However, having to repair damaged property is a naturally following consequence of destructive behavior and so may help the adolescent learn something about the effects of his or her actions. It is always possible that he or she will enjoy the work of repair and may feel some pride in the finished product. It may be hard for staff to avoid making disparaging comments such as, "Don't look so proud, it wouldn't have needed repairing if you hadn't lost your temper." However, residential staff who are alert to opportunities to respond in ways that will maximize opportunities for residents to experience themselves differently will be able to discuss the seriousness of the destructive behavior while at the same time acknowledging the success of the adolescent's efforts at repair. In the long run, feeling good about what he or she has been able to achieve is more likely to lead to responsible and successful behavior than is being humiliated or lectured about failure.

One older adolescent in our program continually went out for the evening and would return obviously, and noisily, drunk. This was clearly unacceptable, and we resorted to a variety of attempts to respond to this behavior. We gave lectures about the evils of alcohol, we tried to appeal to his sense of fairness in terms of his behavior's effect on other residents who were awakened by his return to the house, we expressed our anger and disappointment, and we imposed consequences such as not allowing him out. All of these strategies had no noticeable effect, and the behavior continued.

One night, he arrived back well after midnight obviously drunk. We welcomed him into the unit, asked briefly about his evening, and allowed him to go to bed. He seemed a little perplexed by our (lack of) reaction. The following morning, his headache and hangover were consequence enough!

Of course, our response did not lead to an immediate change in his behavior (and we received a degree of criticism from outside agencies who believed we should have discharged him), yet his hangover was a far more real consequence than any we could have devised. Of course, we did not go out of our way to "protect" his headache the following morning, expressing nonchalant surprise when he complained about the volume of the radio!

— "Crossroads," Wyong Medium Term Accommodation Project,
Wyong, New South Wales

In this example, the reactions of staff had become predictable and had no effect whatsoever on the boy's behavior. The adolescent had had years of practice at becoming immune to such outbursts from adults. Paradoxically, the staff members' lectures and expressions of outrage had become a bigger "headache" than that caused by the alcohol. This meant that his annoyance at peoples' reactions probably obscured his experience of the natural consequence of his behavior. The different response of staff was important both because it was different and because it allowed the natural consequence to operate. (Of course, it was important that his complaints the following day about his headache were not greeted with lectures but responded to in as matter-of-fact a way as possible). The staff were at pains to point out, as they shared this example, that this is not always the way they would respond in such situations. For some young people, it would be appropriate that they respond more firmly. No single response is appropriate for every type of behavior. Certainly, with this young man, the staff had become caught in "more of the same" responses that were both not working and obscuring the natural consequences.

Even Arbitrary Punishment Can Be Framed Meaningfully

On occasion, there is no obvious natural consequence for misbehavior, and an arbitrary penalty has to be imposed. However, again it is crucial to consider how we think about the imposing of the punishment. We may simply make it something unpleasant ("to teach him or her a lesson!"), or we may find ways of carrying it through that make it meaningful in terms of highlighting strength and competence.

Jimmy, age 12, had been admitted following a history of disruptive behavior. His behavior in the unit was variable, although he showed increasing self-control on some occasions. Following a particular outburst, he was told that he would have to go to bed half an hour early as a consequence. Bedtime was normally nine o'clock. Later that day, 8:30 p.m. passed yet staff did nothing to enforce this punishment. At nine o'clock, Jimmy was sent to bed with the other residents.

The following day, one of the staff took Jimmy aside and said, "Jimmy, you were supposed to go to bed half an hour early last night. It seems that you weren't able to take care of doing that, so tonight it will have to be 40 minutes early. Now, do you think you will be feeling enough in control of yourself to get yourself to bed at 8:20, or do you think we will need to make sure that you do it?"

During the evening, a staff member asked Jimmy, "How strong are you feeling?" but nothing more was said. Jimmy took himself to bed early—not 40 minutes early, but sufficiently early to show that he was implementing his own consequence.

— Timaru Hostel, Care Force Youth Services, Sydney

Going to bed early was clearly an arbitrary, imposed punishment that did not bear any obvious relationship to the particular piece of misbehavior. To have forced Jimmy to bed early the first night would have ensured that the punishment was carried out, but would have provided little opportunity for him to think differently about himself. Staff believed that Jimmy's view of himself was that he had little self-control (and he had had lots of professional reinforcement of the view that he was "impulsive"). Accordingly, their concern was that enforcing the punishment would confirm to Jimmy that staff could control his behavior but might reinforce his belief about his own failure at self-control. By making it clear that the punishment would not be ignored, the staff created a context in which Jimmy could think about himself, and experience himself, as having success in self-control.

Of course, had he again failed to carry out this punishment, they would have taken steps to enforce it the following day rather than allow the situation to escalate. They would have done so firmly but, at the same time, would have talked with Jimmy about how hard he was finding it to control his own behavior. They might have discussed with him how he thought they could help him practice self-control, while they remained even more diligent in looking for any small signs of self-control that they could point out to him and discuss.

THE PUNISHMENT MUST FIT THE PERSON, NOT FIT THE CRIME

My object all sublime

I shall achieve in time,

To let the punishment fit the crime, the punishment fit the crime . . .

—*"The Mikado,"* Act II, Gilbert & Sullivan

The Mikado's sentiment in Gilbert and Sullivan's comic opera is familiar. As a parent, I have found myself wondering if the punishment meted out to one of my children was sufficiently commensurate with the severity of the misdemeanor. If swearing at mother means no TV for a night, should fighting in the street mean no TV for three nights or a week? However, before we get too carried away with this debate, we should remember that, in *The Mikado*, these words were spoken (or sung) in reference to the guidelines to be adopted by the Lord High Executioner.

The punishment designed to fit the crime was beheading! Capital punishment is about the *only* way to ensure that misdeeds never recur. Tempting though the prospect may be at times, it is not usually a strategy available to residential staff!

The aim of discipline is that the young person involved should be able to see the possibility of behaving differently, of experiencing success and competence. One of our main principles is that experiencing the possibility of successful or different behavior is more helpful, in the long term, than experiencing the displeasure of problem behavior.

"Intuitive" logic may say that the punishment must fit the crime, but the experience of therapy suggests that the most important ingredient of any intervention designed to bring about change is that it should fit the unique experience of the person involved. What may be meaningful for one person may, in the light of their view of themselves influenced by past experiences of discipline, be oppressive for another. The punishment may fit the crime in some "objective" terms, yet, to a particular young person, it may help ideas of hopelessness and failure persist, and so may not help introduce new ideas about behavior.

A "natural consequence" of property destruction might be that the resident has to pay for the damage or repair it. At first, this seems an appropriate response, and one that will ensure that the resident learns something about responsibility for his or her behavior. However, for some young people, such a demand would be too great a burden. In the context of a history of a sense of hopelessness, the resulting inability to pay for the property or lack of success in repairing it may contribute to further experience of failure. Not only will this mean that the resident has been unable to gain any new information about competence and control, but also the frustration at this failure may well result in further outbursts or refusal to cooperate. Thus, the situation becomes yet another experience of hopelessness, and the opportunity to use it as part of the process of discovering different possibilities is lost.

On the other hand, the consequence of damage might be that the resident has to contact the maintenance department of the agency to report the damage and request that it be repaired. This may appear a trivial response, but it may be an opportunity for the resident to take responsibility for his behavior and its effects in a way that is achievable and not punitive. It also provides a less hostile climate in which staff may discuss with the resident how he will go about making the report and later compliment him for having been able to take responsibility for doing so. Thus, a piece of "problem behavior" may provide an "exception," which may be responded to. With appropriate forewarning of *cooperative maintenance personnel, the person who comes to repair the property may seek the assistance of the resident concerned and may be able to have a useful conversation during the process.*

—adapted from Simes & Trotter, 1990.*

Resisting the temptation to become engrossed with reactions such as "that was no punishment—he got away with it!" tests our resolve to respond to misbehavior in a way that enhances new ideas and experiences rather than simply to react punitively. No consequence is too trivial if it provides new information.

Fourteen-year-old Louise was pretending to go to school, but truanting. She then decided to leave school, found a great apprenticeship to a hair-dresser, but was sacked after a few days because of her inconsistent effort. She (supposedly) changed to the local school, attended a few days, seemed to improve, but truanted again.

It was obvious she preferred to work, so staff voiced their support for this, if she was sure that was what she really wanted. Her mother was prepared to give her permission for a school exemption if she could be committed to her choice of job.

We used the idea of a plane taking off. There is a point down the runway where the pilot is committed to take-off. At that point, if the plane does not either go up or terminate and return to the hangar, it will "crash and burn" (Top Gun movie jargon for failing in a big way) at the end of the runway.

Staff discussed with Louise the dilemma of taking off with her plans for independence, being fully committed to doing it correctly (applying for school exemption, finding a job, and keeping it by hard work) or going back to the hangar (back to school for more preparation). Failure to commit either way would lead to messy problems—crash and burn (truancy officer and school on her back, mother threatening to withdraw financial support, being further behind in school work). She seemed to be keen to avoid the fate of "crash and burn," and there was evidence that she was beginning to see herself as capable of this.

The major difficulty staff experienced as they sought to help Louise work on cleaning up the "messes" she had already created was her

---

*Simes and Trotter have written an extremely helpful paper about ways of dealing with violent behavior in the residential program, and I have adapted a number of their ideas in the remainder of this chapter. The program they write about was one residential unit in an agency to which I consulted for some time, which sought to use the kind of framework set out in this book.

apparent inability to tell the truth. How to deal with this was the major challenge for the staff. They were aware of their responsibility for Louise's safety and so felt that they needed to know where she was and what she was doing. However, they realized that checking up on her, catching her out when she lied, and seeking to impose consequences for this simply made it more likely that she would say nothing or would work harder on her deceit.

Staff tried to find a way to frame this differently by suggesting to Louise that perhaps she was out of the habit of telling the truth. She was asked about her various requests to go out, and to rate them on a scale from 1 to 10, where 1 meant she didn't really care about going and 10 represented wanting badly to go. She agreed that, the closer a specific request was to 10, the more likely she was to lie about the nature or place of the activity. She admitted to developing this pattern with her mother, who would deny her "fun," so she assumed that asking permission from staff (if she told the truth) would get the same "no" response.

Staff suggested that, whenever Louise wanted permission for some activity, they would ask her to rate it on the same scale, and they would take her rating (how badly she wanted to go) into consideration when deciding on their response. They explained that there would be times when their concern for her safety would lead them to say "no"; however, this arrangement might be a way for Louise to start working with the staff, not against them. This would mean that she would be working on saying "no" to herself on some occasions, and accepting this task was her challenge.

Staff announced to Louise that they would create an "Honesty Zone" in the staff office, where she could come to staff and admit to lying if she had done so. On such occasions, staff would only note the incident and not give Louise any consequences for her deceit. Over time, as trust was built, she was able to come to the Honesty Zone more often and more quickly after lying. While staff made it clear that they were not condoning lying, every time Louise came to the Honesty Zone they were able to highlight her success and strength in practicing being more honest. This process helped her to see that she was capable of telling the truth, and sometimes she even got a "yes" to what she wanted.

— Cornerstone, Presbyterian Social Services, Sydney

Parents often seem to get caught up in responses to their children's lying that do not work, and it is easy for residential staff to do the same. In some situations, it may be appropriate to take a strong stand about a resident's lies. In this situation, however, staff recognized that Louise's lying was a response to her fear, especially with her mother, that all requests would be denied. They felt that she had got to the point where she no longer really saw the possibility of being truthful or of trusting people to be fair. The process they devised fit for Louise's particular situation and the view they felt she had of herself. It achieved a number of things. It offered a "face saving" way out of the impasse, and it provided Louise with an opportunity to experiment with trusting the adults caring for her. In addition, it allowed her to experience herself as being truthful and it allowed staff to acknowledge her lying but still be able to highlight her practice at truthfulness.

The other problem with the notion that the punishment must fit the crime is that it is often staff who suffer more than residents. I have seen many families in which an adolescent has been "grounded" for three days as a result of not coming home on time. When he or she then stays out even later one night, the punishment is grounding for two weeks. In the parents' minds, this misbehavior was more serious and so the punishment must be similarly greater. With many of these situations, however, the effect of this is to make life harder for parents as they have even longer to act as wardens. One of the major factors to be considered in devising punishments or consequences should be whether they are achievable, and whether they lead to the parents or staff suffering more than the young person.

CONSEQUENCES DON'T HAVE TO HURT—THEY HAVE TO MAKE A DIFFERENCE

Natural human instinct is that the consequences of misbehavior must be "unpleasant." They must hurt if they are to deter future misbehavior. Certainly, if we rely on ideas from behavioral theory (where unacceptable behavior is "extinguished" by using punishment), then this idea makes sense.

In a residential program, there are two main problems with this idea. The first is a practical one—it doesn't always work. Many of the children and adolescents who find themselves in residential placements are veterans of repeated and severe punishments. Their efforts to "save face" ("That didn't really hurt!") or their growing resentment ("I'll show him!"), often lead parents into an escalating progression of more and more severe punishments. It is easy, and understandable, for residential staff to become caught in similar cycles, yet they seem rarely to make any lasting difference. The second problem relates to what I have suggested about the *purpose* of consequences. If our aim is that the adolescents in our care

should develop a new view of themselves, a view of themselves as successful and competent, then pain is not necessarily conducive to developing
that view. In fact, we might suggest as a general principle, "if in doubt,
underreact."

No punishment or consequence will ensure that a particular behavior
never recurs. The residential placement is a period of trial and error, and
slip ups will not be uncommon. The fact that a resident "re-offends" after
having been given a consequence for misbehavior does *not* mean that the
consequence was not severe enough. It simply means that the process of
learning competence and self-control takes time. Our consequences or
punishments must aim primarily to provide an opportunity for young
people to discover something about themselves and their control.

> *Debbie, age 14, had been admitted after repeated running away,
> fighting, and "irresponsible behavior." In the residential program, she
> alternated between behaving in a cooperative and responsible way and
> behaving in ways that caused tension and disputes between other resi-
> dents. Staff had tried various approaches to her more disruptive epi-
> sodes, including imposing additional household chores as punishment,
> restricting her activities, and monitoring her closely. All these ap-
> proaches often degenerated into further argument or resentment, par-
> ticularly when she failed to cooperate with the consequences.*
>
> *Following an incident in which Debbie again managed to precipitate
> a fight, the staff member on duty said to her, "It seems that you are
> unable to supervise yourself and keep yourself out of trouble at the
> moment. So, we'll have to supervise you until you are feeling ready to
> take over supervising yourself again. So you need to stay with me,
> follow me around for the next couple of hours, and let me know when
> you think you are ready to supervise yourself again."*
>
> *For the next hour and a half, Debbie followed the staff member
> around. This involved sitting outside the office while the staff mem-
> ber attended to some administrative tasks, standing with the staff
> member and watching others play a game, and accompanying the staff
> member shopping. Not all of this was unpleasant (in fact, shopping was
> probably enjoyable), and the staff member did not deliberately seek to
> make Debbie "suffer." After 90 minutes, Debbie was asked if she felt
> ready to resume supervising herself again. When she replied "yes," she
> was asked what made her so sure she would be able to do so, and a
> discussion ensued about those times recently when she had been suc-
> cessful in keeping herself out of trouble and interacting cooperatively.
> She recalled a few such occasions, and the staff member asked her*

how she had managed these. It was agreed that Debbie should resume supervising herself and that she and the staff member would meet briefly in the evening to review how she had done.

— Robinson House, Care Force Youth Services, Sydney

"Close supervision" (where the adolescent must stay with the staff member — *not* where the staff member tags along behind the adolescent!) is often a very effective form of consequence since the meaning of "being supervised vs. supervising oneself" is clear and easily leads to useful discussion. Despite what some might expect, adolescents usually respond to the demand and cooperate, particularly once they "get the hang of it." Of course, if an adolescent does not remain with the staff member as required, this can easily be framed as evidence that he or she is not able to supervise him or herself at the moment and some more stringent restriction may be imposed.

Close supervision is a good example of a consequence that may not involve suffering but may be made meaningful. The important thing is not so much the hour or two that the adolescent spends being supervised but the fact that he or she is able to resume supervision of self afterwards, and it is this to which staff will try to respond.

Keith, age 15, continually did not complete his chores in the unit. Sometimes, he would go for a whole week doing none of the domestic tasks that were allocated to him. Other residents were doing their allotted tasks, and they and the staff were increasingly frustrated with Keith's apparent laziness or uncooperativeness. However, staff recognized that his apparent intransigence was most likely to be exacerbated if they were to impose punishments or engage in "heavy" lectures. Moreover, a common practice in this unit was to impose additional chores as consequences for misbehavior, and it was clear that to impose extra chores as the consequence for refusal to do chores would be self-defeating.

The staff knew he was actually capable of carrying out his tasks, since there had been occasions on which he had done so, and they discussed a different way of framing this impasse. They suggested to Keith that the problem was his difficulty in getting organized to carry out the tasks rather than a refusal to do so. They suggested that, for a week, the staff would do all his chores for him — however, he had to organize them to do so, show them how to do the tasks, and take full responsibility for getting them done. Somewhat bemused, Keith agreed to this and the staff undertook all his allotted duties, at his direction, for a week. They were careful not to complain or make comment, apart from comment about Keith's ability to organize them and his ability to take responsibility for the tasks.

On occasion, however, staff members took this procedure to the extreme. One day, Keith was telling one staff member how to mop the floor, and she was doing so according to his direction. As she finished, she asked him, "So now what?" He replied, "Now you tip the water out." Carrying out his instructions diligently, she tipped the water out— there and then, onto the floor, and claimed confusion when Keith became exasperated.

Keith decided that it would be easier to do the chores himself, and seemed to take pride in being able to do them thoroughly and without direction.

— Trigg Hostel, Care Force Youth Services, Sydney

It would have been easy for staff who were determined "to win" to become embroiled in a stand-off with Keith. Dealing with the situation differently required that they put aside their "natural" inclination to think that he was getting off lightly. Their response got the tasks done and still enabled Keith to experience responsibility for their completion, which would establish the possibility of his continuing this responsibility in a different way thereafter.

MEANINGFUL CONSEQUENCES MAY ACTUALLY BE FUN!

As I have suggested above, suffering is not necessarily a condition for learning and may in fact be counterproductive. Sometimes an episode of misbehavior lends itself to a consequence that entails a new experience in quite a pleasant manner.

Three older adolescent boys engaged in constant bickering. It seemed that they could not be in one another's presence without some type of fight developing, and they continued to "invade" each other's bedrooms in taunting and annoying ways. Separating them worked for a while, but its effects were usually short-lived.

After one typical episode in which a fight developed, the staff member on duty told them that they were immediately to go and play three games of pool together. She knew that they all enjoyed playing pool. The boys' reaction to this consequence was, "Is that all you are going to do to us?" The staff member firmly insisted they go and play their games of pool. They did so and seemed to enjoy themselves.

After the three games of pool, the staff member sat down with the boys and complimented them for having been able to enjoy physical proximity without becoming aggressive. She contrasted this with their earlier behavior, which had suggested that they were not able to handle such physical closeness, and wondered how they had been able to manage it during the games of pool.

— Trigg Hostel, Care Force Youth Services, Sydney

Again, what is important in this example is the *meaning* that was given to the consequence. At first, the boys thought the "punishment" was a joke. Had it not been followed up afterwards, it might have been. However, the consequence itself was simply a way to engineer a situation that might lead to the boys' experiencing themselves interacting differently and would provide useful material to be discussed with them afterwards.

A staff member who was preoccupied with "teaching them a lesson" (in the traditional sense) would not have been able to take the risk involved in administering such a consequence. However, the fact that they enjoyed this experience and were then able to discuss it sensibly led to their learning a far better lesson that they otherwise might.

DEALING WITH EXTREME BEHAVIOR

Of course, there will be times when the seriousness of misbehavior — violence or persistent disruptiveness, for example — may resist all attempts at creative and meaningful management. Even at these times, however, it is important to consider how we think about such occasions. To think of the adolescent concerned as "resistant" or as "deliberately trying to sabotage his or her placement" (normal and understandable though such thoughts may be) is unlikely to be helpful in helping staff deal with the situation. We may still assume that the behavior is a reflection of the way that the young person views him or herself, and we may seek to deal with it in such a way as to provide the possibility of the young person gaining new information about him or herself.

Simes and Trotter (1990) write of a residential program where the older adolescent boys, often court-referred, had histories of violence and abuse and where violent outbursts were not uncommon. They write that, even in extreme situations, the goal is still that the young person should be able to experience taking control of himself.

Staff will seek to respond to the young person in ways that *suggest* that they believe him to be capable of taking control. They will ask him to move outside until he is able to calm himself down. Of course, a young person in the midst of a violent outburst may not hear (or may not appear to hear) such comments, however this attitude of allowing space for him to regain control is potentially powerful.

Being calm and not acting in ways that escalate the situation are, of course, important and are considered in the ways that staff members respond. "I will wait for you to get back in control" (which has the implicit message of "I know you *will* get back in control") is preferable to "If you keep being out of control, I will stop you." We aim to give the young person as much time and space as possible to enable him to make a decision to regain control.

Staff seek to avoid stepping in with physical control, both because it is difficult to implement and because it may contribute to [views of self of] dependency and helplessness—"I am uncontrollable; someone else needs to control me"—and denies the young person the opportunity to experience controlling himself. Staff need to be aware of their own self-control in resisting these invitations to step in. Only when staff or residents are in imminent danger, or extensive physical damage is occurring, would we intervene physically. (Simes & Trotter, 1990, p. 58)

Sometimes, it is most expedient to move other residents and staff to safety and give the particular adolescent time to cool down. Then, once this has occurred, staff can discuss with the adolescent concerned (and with the others who may have witnessed the outburst) not only the seriousness of such violent behavior but also the fact that he or she was able to take control eventually. In keeping with the principles discussed above, it can be very powerful to convey the message, "Violent behavior is unacceptable (and there may have to be some consequence for it), but we are impressed that you were able to take control of yourself more quickly this time than you have done in the past. How were you able to do this?" The episode itself is not ignored, but it may still provide an opportunity for success to be discussed. To be able to think that he or she has been able to make some progress in self-control is a far better position in which to be left than to think simply that he or she has failed yet again. Discussing the episode in this way also tends to make it more likely that the resident will cooperate with any consequence that might be given.

Stepping in and Taking Control

Of course, staff's paramount responsibility is for the safety of all residents and staff, and this will sometimes require physical intervention. My experience of a variety of residential programs suggests that this is necessary less often than sometimes imagined. I am sure that staff in some programs intervene with physical restraint primarily because of their own (very real) anxiety about safety rather than because the behavior really warrants it.

It is interesting to note how our attitudes towards violent behavior seem to become self-fulfilling. I once worked in a program where physical restraint of residents displaying out-of-control behavior was a common response. It was not uncommon to walk through the unit and witness someone being restrained or even sat upon by staff (or being given tranquilizing medication). The perceived need for this response became self-perpetuating, since the frequency of violent or out-of-control outbursts became greater as time went on. We might hypothesize that the general message being conveyed was "We will control you" and (by implication) "You are not able to control yourselves." Faced with this regular confirmation of views of lack of control, the children and adolescents continued to display evidence of their lack of control. In the program described above (Simes & Trotter, 1990), however, such extreme outbursts were less frequent despite the fact that the histories of these boys were often more violent than those of the adolescents in the unit in which I worked. It seems that the general stance of staff, demonstrated by their responses to various incidents, suggested the general view that "We believe you are able to take control of your behavior." Within this "climate," these young men seemed to be more likely to behave in ways that confirmed this.

Thus, it is not simply a matter of how staff respond to a particular episode of extreme behavior, but a matter of the information that is conveyed by the general attitude of staff to such occurrences.

When a violent outburst requires intervention, staff need to consider carefully how to intervene. An attempt to take control physically may simply inflame the situation. For all but the largest staff member, seeking to restrain an out-of-control adolescent is a daunting prospect, and a failed attempt is virtually guaranteed to lead to an increase in violence—not just because it makes the adolescent more angry, but because it reinforces the view that this behavior is not controllable, which is frightening for the adolescent as well as for the staff.

Sometimes, it is preferable to involve the police in the situation. This need not be seen as an admission of helplessness on the part of staff, but rather as the natural consequence of destructive behavior or assault. Certainly, the involvement of the police is much more a natural consequence than is being sat upon by staff and/or having tranquilizing medication administered. Any such appearance by the police will have implications for other residents who witness it, and it will be important to discuss it with them later. I know of some programs where the staff have taken time to develop a constructive relationship with the local police. This does not mean that they call on the police often. However, it has meant that the police have offered constructive assistance on those (hopefully rare) occasions when their help has been required.

The consequence of such extreme violence may be that the resident is asked to leave the program for a time (or may be removed by the police). This may be an appropriate consequence for extreme behavior even after it has calmed down. In fact, it is generally preferable to give such a consequence later rather than in the heat of the moment. Some time after the episode, the resident may be told, "You know that we are not able to tolerate continued violence like yesterday's. We are pleased that you were able to settle down and get yourself under control; however, it is not fair to the others to have to cope with such outbursts. We have decided that you will have to leave here for a week so that we have a chance to get the unit settled again. We hope that you will want to come back and to keep working on developing more control over your anger."

I know a couple of residential units that have used such a strategy on rare occasions. They generally worked with the adolescent to help find alternate accommodation for the week (since returning home was not always appropriate) and were prepared to wait a couple of days until an alternative was available. Taking this stance helps make it clear that having to leave is a *consequence* of the behavior and not a "knee-jerk" reaction or punishment, and so may make it more meaningful.

At the end of the prescribed period (which need not be more than a few days), the adolescent may seek to return to the residential program. This, of course, provides an opportunity to discuss the whole issue of control of behavior. He or she can be asked whether or not he/she thinks such behavior is less likely to occur in future and can be invited to review previous evidence of self-control as part of this discussion. It is important that the return be framed as positively as possible and not be seen as "we are prepared to take you back but you are on trial."

Returning in the context of being "on trial" both sets the young person up to fail and also makes it more likely that both adolescent and staff will be alert to evidence of failure rather than success. Some programs, seeking to make the young person's "suspension" from the program as forceful as possible, insist that readmission involve a meeting with a senior person from the program in which the young person agrees to certain conditions or to work on certain issues. This is often seen as helping the young person "take the program seriously" and often includes a period of "probation." Again, my concern is that being asked to leave the program for a period of time is likely to have been an experience of hopelessness or failure and probably will not, in itself, increase motivation to comply. An implicit expectation that the adolescent should now have "learned his lesson" and will not repeat difficult behavior is both unrealistic and likely to be self-defeating. Any context of probation or of agreeing to a "new contract" is likely to make it more difficult for staff to notice and respond to successful behavior or to promote a context of experimentation, since it inevitably orients people's attention to compliance or noncompliance.

The young person's return to the program needs to be framed as an opportunity to continue with previous success and practice. It may involve an agreement to undertake a particular program, which might be designed to provide opportunities to experiment with, or notice, different behavior, but this does not require the "hurdle" of a trial period.

ASKING THE YOUNG PERSON TO LEAVE

Sometimes, behavior has been so intolerable, or infractions of the rules so repeated, that a decision is made that the adolescent must leave the program permanently. In some programs, these events are termed "disciplinary discharges."

Such a decision ought not be taken lightly. As mentioned before, I have seen too many instances where a young person has been "thrown out" of a residential program for displaying the kinds of behavior that led to his or her admission. If we choose to accept adolescents into our program who are in need of "treatment" because they are violent, we cannot precipitously discharge them because they show violent behavior! Such an action will simply confirm views of hopelessness. Of course, this does not mean that we tolerate any and all behavior. Nonetheless, we need to ensure that our expectations are not such that they make such discharges almost inevitable for the more difficult residents.

If we reach a point at which a disciplinary discharge is being considered, it is important that we examine the situation closely. Often, our own responses have contributed to the situation. I'm sure many readers have witnessed a resident being told, "If that happens again, you will have to leave," and then have found that the prophecy becomes self-fulfilling. I well remember a situation where an adolescent had been warned by staff that his consistent refusal to attend school was an indication that he "did not want to continue in the program." Concerned by the apparent harshness of this, I attempted a "therapeutic retreat." I said to him, "You are expected to go to school; however, you will not be thrown out for not doing so. But, if you hit anybody, you will have to leave!" I came out of the interview and, realizing the self-fulfilling prophecy I had established, commented to a coworker, "I give him 24 hours." In fact, it took him only eight hours to hit another resident, forcing us to expel him. We had to follow through on our "threat," but I was left feeling that I had inadvertently made this inevitable.

My observation is that these extreme situations are more likely to occur in programs where the philosophy is one of control. If the context becomes one of staff feeling great responsibility to control the behavior of residents, it is easy for "power struggles" to escalate to a point of no return. Hopefully, before a situation reaches this point, we can stop and consider some completely different way of handling it rather than becoming caught up in doing "more of the same."

Despite these comments, I acknowledge that asking a resident to leave is sometimes necessary. When this is the case, we still need to consider how it is framed. I have witnessed some residential programs where a resident who is being asked to leave is told, "Your behavior shows that you are deciding to leave the program." I suspect that this does not fit with the young person's experience and is an unnecessary (and false) attempt to frame things positively. It is far better to be honest about the fact that the program cannot continue to accommodate the young person while still seeking to frame this positively.

> We want these endings to occur in a positive way for the resident, a way that will open up new choices for them rather than be dominated by a sense of failure. Consequently, we tell the resident of his strengths, abilities and the qualities we have appreciated as well as explaining how his behavior has led us to ask him to leave. (Simes & Trotter, 1990, p. 60)

Again, the aim is that this move should not be seen as punitive. Therefore, the adolescent might be allowed to remain for a short period until alternative arrangements are made — and the discussion about how he or she can ensure that other residents are not in danger during this time can be a very positive one.

BUT OUR CLIENTS ARE YOUNGER CHILDREN

The examples in this chapter are largely from programs dealing with adolescents, and it may seem easier to "take risks" in dealing with adolescents than in work with younger children. Certainly, staff working with younger children have greater responsibilities in terms of care and protection, and their responses must take these into consideration. Nonetheless, staff working with children are equally prone to become caught up in self-defeating reactions to misbehavior.

In my therapy practice, I often see parents who are stuck in repeated patterns of unsuccessful reactions to their eight- or nine-year-old children. They continue to resort to punishments that seem to make no difference. The stakes appear higher and their concern for their children's well-being is understandably greater, yet I have seen numerous examples where allowing natural consequences to operate or simply "doing something different" has been effective.

The specific components of our use of discipline with children may differ from those used with adolescents, but the general principles may similarly be applied.

THAT'S FINE IN THEORY, BUT . . .

I can well imagine readers thinking, "That's fine in theory, but we have ten difficult adolescents to deal with, and we cannot afford the luxury of such creative approaches. When things get difficult, we are doing well just to survive!"

I didn't promise it would be easy, and dealing with misbehavior and difficult outbursts rarely is. However, our aim is more than survival. Our aim is that our work with the children or adolescents in our program should make a difference. What this means is **not** that we have to come up with some fancy way of dealing with every situation. Often, we will deal with misbehavior in ways that are not very different from the ways that we have always done. All this approach asks is that we *think* about discipline and consequences and see them as part of the ongoing process of helping children and adolescents experience new possibilities for behavior and be able to begin to see themselves differently.

As with the examples throughout this book, the particular examples in this chapter are taken from actual residential programs, some of which were dealing with very difficult residents. What they have in common is a determination on the part of the staff to *respond* to behavior meaningfully rather than simply to *react* intuitively.

None of the examples in the chapter, and none of the great ideas you might come up with, can be taken out of context. Responding differently to an episode of misbehavior does not work in isolation. The kinds of responses and consequences I have discussed only work when they are part of the overall way that staff see their role and think about their actions—when they are part of an overall "climate" within a residential unit that seeks to maximize opportunities for new experiences and new possibilities.

9

PARENTS ARE PART
of the PROCESS, TOO

I have commented earlier on the tension that characterizes many residential programs—between the expectation that the program will assume responsibility and "fix" the child on the one hand, and the need to maintain the cooperation and involvement of the parents on the other. All too often have I heard residential staff lament the lack of interest of particular parents or express frustration that parents are undermining the program. However, if parents feel like failures, it is not surprising that they appear uncooperative at times, and we do not need to conclude that they are secretly "rejecting" their child. Various aspects of the residential process—therapy sessions, urgent phone calls to report that the child has absconded, comments about how things are improving, and so on—serve constantly to draw attention to their perceived failure. If a process was going to make you even more aware of the things you had done wrong, would you want to cooperate? This is not to say that staff set out to disempower parents. Rather, the meaning the parents ascribe to the program often serves to confirm their sense of hopelessness.

It is not sufficient, therefore, simply to arrange activities that will involve parents. Without a consideration of the meaning of these activities within the process, they may just provide more opportunities for parents to "prove" their uncooperativeness. A number of parents have described to me their experiences of leaving parent groups feeling despondent or angry. They felt acutely that attention was being drawn to their failings. They could not help but feel, as staff talked about strategies that worked for managing children, that there was an unspoken implication that what they had done before had been wrong.

We need to consider not only the meaning of the problem and the placement, but also the meaning for parents of their involvement. It is quite possible to consider the placement differently, perhaps reframe it in similar ways to those suggested in previous chapters, and then undermine that good work by doing nothing about how we frame our ongoing contact with parents.

In short, everything that happens in the program must be judged according to whether it may further disempower parents. Anything that involves staff appearing to "know better" or telling parents how they should manage their child (or boasting about staff's success where parents failed) runs this risk.

PARENTS CAN GIVE US USEFUL ADVICE

While presenting a workshop in an Australian regional center recently, I was interviewed by a local newspaper and asked what my main point was. The reporter seemed skeptical as I discussed concentrating on people's strengths and resources rather than focusing on problems or pathology and asked me about how I approached "inadequate parents" or "dysfunctional families." When I replied that I thought most parents managed things well most of the time, she was shocked. "You can't tell me that you really believe that!" she exclaimed.

As I have said, whether we approach our work as a search for problems or as a recognition of strength is ultimately an arbitrary choice. However, I have found that if we treat parents as if we believe they are competent, they are more likely to be so.

However we look at it, the parents know their child far better than we do. It may be true that they have become stuck in a particular pattern of parent-child interaction that is not working, but that does not mean that it is helpful to regard them as incompetent. Seeking their advice as to how we should deal with their child is not only a useful technique in our therapeutic endeavors, it might also prove to help us.

Williamson Street, a unit for adolescent boys, was previously little more than a hostel, a form of alternative accommodation. More recently, the program has adopted a much more explicit family focus. This has had various practical manifestations, such as all staff now being called "family workers" rather than "youth workers" or "residential staff." However, the main difference has been in how the staff think about what their purpose is and how they can operate the program in a way that maximizes the likelihood of parents feeling valued and competent.

When a young person is referred for admission, staff make it clear that Williamson Street is not a place for teenagers to live. "Your son lives at home—although it may be helpful for him to stay here some nights of the week." They do not offer full-time placement—the adolescent lives at home at least one night of the week. That is, workers are clear that they do not assume the parenting role, and they do not wish the unit to assume the role of "home." In keeping with this, and in contrast to many residential programs, they actively discourage the adolescents from bringing posters, favorite possessions and so on to make their rooms feel "like home." Residents are expected just to bring those things they will need for a few days' stay away from home, much as would happen if they were sleeping over at a friend's house. Sometimes, in fact, adolescents will find that they return from time at home to a different room within the unit.

"Your kid is still your kid. Any decision that would normally be made by parents will still be made by you," the staff tell parents. So, for example, parents might be asked to specify the bedtime for their child (within broad parameters of what is acceptable within the program). If the child does not comply with this "rule," staff will telephone parents and ask them how they would like the situation to be handled. Parents, of course, may not know how it should be dealt with, in which case staff may say, "We can tell you some of the things other parents have told us have been helpful in dealing with such situations." In fact, they sometimes tell parents, "The decisions will be made by you, to the extent that you might get sick of us calling you to ask your advice."

My questions to the staff were how the residents coped with different rules for different adolescents, and what they did about those cases where parents could not agree to having the child home for even one night per week.

In response to the first question, they replied that the staff had (initially, at least) experienced more problems with the fact of different rules than had the residents. If an adolescent complained that, "I have to go to bed at 9 o'clock, but some kids are allowed to stay up until 10 o'clock," staff would reply, "Well, that's the rule your parents set. How do you usually go about negotiating things with your parents? Would you like to talk about how you could discuss this with your parents when you go home at the weekend, or should we ask them to come in for a discussion before then?" Thus, young person and parents are left in the position of having control over the day-to-day things that often cause friction.

In answer to the second question, the staff have found that once parents understand that their competence is being affirmed rather than a group of workers taking over their responsibilities, it has been rare for parents to refuse to have their adolescent at home for even one night. In fact, many of the residents are spending more nights at home than in the residential unit.* When, for whatever reason, parents feel unable to have the child home for even one night of the week, staff will work with parents to find an alternative place for the child or adolescent to stay on these nights.

Parents are involved as much as possible in every aspect of the program. Instead of simply inviting parents to visit for a meal, it is more likely that parents will bring part of the meal, and the staff and residents will prepare the other part. Staff commented that this often allows the adolescents a chance to be proud of their parents in front of other residents. Previously, staff would arrange outings for residents. Now, they will either help negotiate parents' taking their adolescent out for the afternoon, or arrange an outing and invite parents to join them (and allow them as much responsibility for their own child as possible).

Allied to this more explicit family focus in the way the residential program operates, is a greater intensity of family counseling during the adolescent's stay. The fact that the adolescent continues, from the beginning, to have at least one night per week away from the residential unit means that family counseling can realistically have a focus on the ways that family members are experimenting in the "more normal" nonresidential environment.

—St. Luke's Family Care, Bendigo, Victoria

This example is not intended to be "the model" for how residential programs should operate. It may be inappropriate for a number of situations, and it raises various questions. Nonetheless, it is an impressive example of a program that has seriously considered the meaning, not just of particular activities, but of the whole structure of the program and has sought to frame everything in ways that affirm parents' expertise. It is not surprising that parents are more likely to be cooperative with such a program. Of course, it would be easier for staff simply to deal with difficulties

---

*Of course, given the vagaries of the funding of residential programs, this unit is quite likely to lose its funding, since the adolescents are spending more time at home than in the unit, and so bed-occupancy rates are low. It is an unfortunate fact in our field that programs are usually funded not to be successful!

as they arise. Seeking parental advice makes it more complicated. How-ever, involving parents in this manner means that they are being equipped for the kinds of situations that will arise after the placement has finished. Staff's role is to assist and facilitate negotiation and problem-solving while parents have the opportunity to experience themselves as having success, under more "controlled" conditions.

Some years ago, I was involved with four young children who had been removed from their mother's care. The case plan specified that the aim was to return them to their mother but that she needed "help with parenting skills" before this could occur. As part of the residential program, it was suggested that the mother would visit the unit two afternoons each week so that she could learn from the staff techniques for managing her children. She agreed to this willingly. However, after a few weeks, she began to cooperate less with the plan—her car would often break down on the designated afternoons, or she would report an urgent appointment, or she would simply not turn up. Some staff began to question her "real" desire to have her children returned to her care. At the same time, she seemed to become less willing to report any difficulties she experienced during the children's weekend visits home. Staff gleaned from the children that all was not going smoothly during these visits, and that she often left them with other people rather than manage them herself. The therapist was anxious to use this information in therapy sessions as a means of discussing alternate strategies with her. She appeared to become more "resistant" to therapy and to demon-strate "denial" of the difficulties.

Eventually, the therapist said to the mother, "As you know, we have had a couple of staff changes in the unit, so we have one or two staff members who do not know your children. We wonder if you would be willing to visit the unit two afternoons each week to show the staff how best to manage your children." She willingly agreed and, even though what actually happened during her visits was little different from what had occurred before, she rarely missed a scheduled afternoon from then on. She also began to be much more open about the difficulties she faced and her fears about having her children home, which were able to be discussed in a more cooperative manner.

The context of having to prove her parenting skills in order to have her children returned was disempowering in itself. The process of attending the unit to be "taught" by staff was inevitably experienced as focusing on her deficiencies and was an excellent way to "create" resistance or denial. It is not difficult to see how this scenario could have perpetuated a vicious cycle in which her behavior was increasingly seen as evidence of her "real, underlying rejection" of her children, which would lead to her behaving more and more in ways that would confirm this view. The children might well have ended up not being returned to their mother—not because of any deficiencies on her part, but because of the effects of the way the whole situation had been framed.

Framing her involvement differently, asking her advice and so affirming her competence, involved only a small change in the practical aspects of the program. Nonetheless, it was a major change in the meaning of the process for mother and children.

WHOSE CHILDREN ARE THEY?

When children or adolescents enter a residential program, parents are often asked to sign a multitude of forms giving consent for the residential staff to take responsibility for the child. It may seem like a complete handover of parental responsibility, almost a resignation from the position of parent. It is hardly surprising that, once we have accepted parents' resignations, they sometimes do not appear to want to cooperate with our efforts to involve them. Further, I am not sure that accepting their resignation is a good way to begin a process that aims to have them take up the position again in the future.

Thinking about the meaning of even apparently minor administrative or procedural matters, may make a difference.

> In Australia, parents receive a twice-monthly payment from the government ("family allowance") for each child. Technically, if a child is placed apart from the family, the particular agency can claim this payment instead of the parents, and some agencies ask parents to complete the appropriate forms to allow this to happen. Many units use this payment to allow them to give an "allowance" to the children or adolescents in residence and often have a weekly ritual of handing out a certain sum of money to each child and then depositing the remainder in the child's bank account or retaining some of it to help defray expenses. Some residential programs, however, have now encouraged parents to retain the family allowance payment but to provide the weekly allowance to their child themselves. This may lead to more complicated negotiation between staff and parents, but it allows parents to retain some of their own responsibilities and so their sense of continued involvement with their child.

It may be administratively smoother for payments to be centralized, and this would avoid having to deal with parents who forget or are late in giving their child his or her allowance. However, administrative smoothness is rarely a good indicator of the extent to which a procedure affirms parents.

When a child becomes ill or sustains an injury, staff of a residential program have obvious responsibilities to ensure adequate medical treatment, and their awareness of these responsibilities may overshadow their willingness to think about the implications for parents' views. However, this is a time when parental responsibility may also be heightened (since, in times of illness, other frustrations and "grudges" are more easily put aside). The simple action of staff telephoning parents to advise them of the injury and seek their advice, perhaps allowing (or even asking) them to take their child or adolescent to the doctor or hospital, may make a great difference in the parents' feeling of maintaining involvement and responsibility for their child.

These are only two examples, but they demonstrate that it is important that we consider even the seemingly mundane aspects of our interaction with parents as we think about the meanings we create. Parenting is characterized by these kinds of day-to-day experiences. If the residential unit (in the interests of efficiency) assumes responsibility for such events, this may simply reinforce parents' experience of having their power superseded. The more we can involve them in their child's life, the more likely they are to be able and willing to have the child return home.

Helping Parents Feel Part of the Process of Change

In some residential units, parents are aware that a therapeutic program of some sort operates but they are not clear about its details. From their point of view, it is a little like putting their child or adolescent into some mysterious "black box." They don't know much about what goes on in there, and they simply wait for the child to emerge at the other end of the process.

If our aim is that the residential treatment will help young person and parents view themselves as competent and hence able to continue to live together, it is imperative that parents feel that they are more than just passive observers of the process. If we want them to be able to respond differently to steps that their child makes, we must find ways of helping them feel part of the process of those steps occurring.

- When a resident behaves differently or shows a small "step forward," when staff are responding to an exception, they might suggest that the child or adolescent phone his or her parents to tell them about the success. It is preferable that the therapist or residential staff discuss with parents at the beginning of the admission that this will happen and ask parents if they would be happy to have their child report to them in this way. Forewarned, they are less likely to dismiss the news when they receive the call. We must bear in mind that parents may be unprepared for receiving calls about their child's successes. Often, the only time they expect to receive phone calls from the unit (similar to their experience with calls from a child's school) is when there is a problem.

- As events occur or issues arise during the program, it will sometimes be appropriate for staff to discuss with the resident how he or she might go about letting parents know about them, or suggest that the resident might seek parental advice.

- Involving parents in some activities or outings, or inviting them to meals in the unit, are opportunities to help them feel part of the process. It is preferable that these not simply be opportunities for them to be visitors or observers but that staff find ways to help them feel involved (such as the example above of parents contributing food to a meal). If some "incident" occurs while the parents are present, it may be unhelpful for staff to "spring into action" to deal with it, leaving the parent feeling powerless. Rather, their advice may be sought or they may be asked if they wish to deal with their son or daughter themselves. Of course, pushing them to do so may be equally unhelpful if they feel incapable of doing so, but at least offering the opportunity may be important. (I have witnessed some units, often those with apparently complicated therapeutic programs, where staff are worried that parents might handle a situation in a way that compromises the integrity of the program. If we reach a point where the details of the program become more important than the experience of the people with whom we work, then perhaps we should reassess what we think we are aiming to achieve!)

- Many programs use small "ritual celebrations" to highlight particular steps a resident has achieved. Inviting parents to attend these, perhaps even to participate, is a way to help them feel part of the process of change. It avoids their feeling that, as discharge approaches, evidence of their child's change is suddenly being "sprung upon" them.

Where residents return home for weekend leave, the times they are collected or returned by their parents offer crucial opportunities for engaging parents. In programs where the majority of residents spend weekends at home, Friday evening when they are collected and Sunday evening when they are returned are often times when fewer staff are rostered on duty. The rationale seems to be that there is little "therapeutic" work to be done and that the practical coordination of comings and goings can be achieved by fewer staff. This may be a mistake. Despite the inevitable chaos that surrounds children leaving or returning, the informal encounters between parents and staff can be more than just an exchange of factual information or negotiation about the time of return.

With sufficient staff present, there is opportunity for them to take time to think about the implications of their discussions with parents.

- A simple conversation about what plans the family has for the weekend might become, "So, you're going to visit friends. Will Daniel be playing with other children there? Well, that might be a good opportunity to practice some of the things he's been doing here about getting on with people. It would be really helpful if you could keep a lookout for any small signs that he is taking steps to get on differently with people." In some ways, it is not important whether or not Daniel actually practices behaving differently. Rather, this comment reorients his parents' attention. Because of previous experiences, they might naturally be alert for any examples of problem behavior. The request that they look out for different behavior — for exceptions — may help them approach the weekend more hopefully, although it is important to avoid suggesting utopian expectations of the child. If they notice different behavior, they will respond differently, and any emerging changes are more likely to continue.

- If a child has some graphic record of success at the unit (such as a "beating my temper" chart, or the "Growing Up Dial" from Chapter 7), the child can be encouraged to show this to the parent who comes to collect him or her, and a staff member might make some brief comment.

- When parents return their child or adolescent at the end of the weekend, the staff member might simply inquire, "How did things go this weekend?" If they experience this as a genuine enquiry, parents are more likely to be able to nominate one or two events that were successful over the weekend. Of course, it is even better for the staff member to ask, "What went better this weekend?" which may make it more likely that parents will remember small successes. Not only does this give staff information they may use during the week, but it affirms the parents' competence and allows them to finish the weekend feeling more hopeful about success continuing.

What is important about these examples is that they are not suggesting mini-therapy sessions but rather that staff members seek to make their exchanges with parents meaningfully focused on success. Many of the families with whom we work are stuck in feelings of hopelessness, and it is this, more than any specific aspects of the problem behavior, that works against treatment being successful. Beginning or ending the weekend feeling even a little more hopeful is more likely to lead to change occurring and being noticed.

> *Working with parents was always important to us since we recognized that, however "creative" our work with residents was, everything could fail if parents had not been able to see things differently. We sought to foster a climate where parents felt free to visit the unit whenever they liked, and these contacts were often more fruitful than any structured meetings. We encouraged parents to stay for meals—the afternoons they came for family therapy sessions were often good opportunities for this—and to participate in the domestic activities of the unit.*
>
> *Many of the parents with whom we worked had been identified by the welfare authorities as "requiring input into parenting and domestic skills." However, we soon learned that our efforts to "teach" them seemed to go unheeded or even helped foster antagonism. We recognized that many of the skills in which they had been identified as deficient were activities that formed part of our day-to-day program anyway. The young people in the unit took part in meal preparation and often accompanied us shopping, so it was natural for us to discuss these matters with them. When parents visited, we tried to involve them in such discussions and would seek their advice as to how to assist their child in preparing food and so on. In this way, they were able to be part of their child achieving practical success and were able to enjoy a pleasant parent-child interaction around the activity. Moreover, they were able to help develop their "parenting and domestic skills" in a participatory process that helped them feel affirmed.*
>
> *Similarly, we would often telephone parents and discuss with them a consequence we were planning to give to their child. Again, they were able to feel valued and included, while at the same time having an opportunity to think about discipline in a slightly different way.*
>
> *—Robinson House, Care Force Youth Services, Sydney*

This example represents only a relatively minor change in how staff managed things—but it created the potential for a huge difference in how parents experienced their involvement.

Involving Parents in the Day-to-Day
Difficulties of the Program

In our residential work with young people, there are inevitably times when the unit seems to get out-of-control or staff feel that they did not handle things well. It is tempting to try to hide these occurrences from the parents of the young people with whom we are working, perhaps due to the fear on our part that *they* might fear that we do not really know what we are doing. However, such occurrences are exactly the kinds of experiences that parents are going to have as they continue with their children (and have had in the past), and they may learn a great deal from sharing such frustrations with us.

> *This unit had six young people in residence, some of whom were new and a couple of whom were struggling with issues about temper and control. The unit was in one of its "less quiet" periods! One of the issues that kept emerging (and growing) was that of curfew. Some of the adolescents were coming back late and breaking windows in order to gain admittance to the unit. Staff quickly became caught up in trying to enforce the curfew by seeking to impose consequences for infractions, while the residents became more and more creative and determined in their efforts to circumvent it.*
>
> *Within this overall atmosphere, a particular incident occurred one evening. One resident was having temper outbursts in the house and, in an effort to allow him to take control, staff asked him to go outside to cool down. He refused to come back inside and subsequently broke into another building. Mindful of not wanting to repeat earlier impasses, staff members decided not to try to force him out. We framed this as him deciding he needed to isolate himself as a way of helping himself calm down, and we offered him blankets, and told him we would wait until he felt ready to return.*
>
> *This seemed a helpful way to deal with the situation and avoid a fruitless power struggle, until the other five adolescents decided to join him. All six residents were now "camping" in the other building. Again, we decided that any efforts on our part to take control would lead to a full-scale siege, so we waited. After two or three nights, the residents became alarmed when they thought they heard an intruder and so returned to the unit. However, they continued to "camp out" together in the common area. During the day, the unit operated as normal, but each night, the residents refused to return to their own rooms. We decided not to step in, since we felt this would not be helpful, despite increasing pressure from parents who were hearing about the situation from their children. We assured them that we were checking regularly*

on the safety of everyone involved and that we were sure the residents would end this stand-off when they felt ready to do so. After a week of this situation, the residents cleaned the room and returned their bedding to their own rooms.

We now faced a dilemma. We felt that our not stepping in had been the most helpful response but thought that some action still needed to be taken. There had been various incidents leading up to the situation, and a number of the consequences that had been imposed as a result of these incidents had not been done. We felt that the various consequences ought to be performed, but we wanted to do this in a way that did not lead to further confrontation.

Finally, we decided to invite the parents and the residents to a "Consequences Games Night" and told the residents that this would be an evening for catching up on consequences. We divided the group into teams, each with two adolescents, their parents, and one staff member, and talked with the group about how this was an opportunity for us all to practice supporting each other and helping each other. There were consequences that needed doing, but by supporting each other in doing them, we might all learn something.

Each "consequence" was drawn from a box and announced to the group. The incidents that each consequence referred to were explained anonymously; however, it was not uncommon in the context of the evening for the particular adolescent concerned to call out, "Yes, that was me." The teams then had a race to see which team could complete the consequence most quickly and creatively.

The first drawn was a consequence for continued difficulty recognizing the physical boundaries of the unit (that is, absconding, breaking into the other building, and so on). The consequence was that each team was given timber and ropes and had to build a fence around the unit, complete with signs that made clear the meaning of the boundary. The second consequence was a team "fire drill" as a consequence for continued smoking problems. Others were in the same vein.

At the end of the evening, a celebratory supper marked the fact that consequences had been completed and people had been able to have fun while doing this. The parents were much more positive about the program, and a number of them spent quite some time discussing with staff different ways of handling things. Initially, parents could not understand our approach to dealing with their adolescents' behavior. "Why don't you just stop my son smoking?" one mother demanded. When we asked how she thought we should do this, she replied, "Well, I just wrestle him to the ground and take his cigarettes from him." Others of the parents had few strategies other than physical punishment.

We were clear that we did not expect parents necessarily to adopt the exact strategies we had used, and we told them that the consequences evening was not the way we would usually deal with this situation. Nonetheless, it created an atmosphere where parents were open to thinking about the meaning of discipline, and they were able to comment to us that, even though the consequences had been fun, they had been able to witness their children taking responsibility for their behavior.

—Robinson House, Care Force Youth Services, Sydney

HARNESSING PARENTS' MOTIVATION

When parents do appear uncooperative or oppositional, it is easy to become stuck in a response either of trying harder and harder to engage them or of dismissing them as unable to offer anything helpful. We need constantly to remind ourselves that their apparent opposition may make perfect sense in terms of the view they have of themselves, their child, and the situation. From their point of view, they have endured longstanding "abuse" from their adolescent and/or from professionals.

Just as we can employ reframing to offer a way of talking about a situation that might make it more likely that an adolescent will be "motivated," so we can use the same technique with parents. This is not a matter of "being manipulative" in order somehow to engineer their cooperation. Rather, it entails a recognition that any situation can validly be viewed from a variety of perspectives and, if we choose to look for more positive explanations of attitude and behavior, we are much more likely to find a way of engaging defeated parents.

Despite the school's longstanding complaints about 11-year-old William's extreme temper tantrums, which eventually led to his exclusion from school and his admission to a residential child-psychiatry unit, William's parents appeared to deny or "downplay" the seriousness of the problem. They claimed that the school simply did not manage the children properly. Within the unit, staff certainly experienced William's tantrums and their sometimes great difficulty getting him under control was exacerbated by his parents' continuing assertions that they had never seen these tantrums. In an effort to "prove" the situation to William's parents, staff instituted a plan whereby the parents would be called whenever William had such an outburst. Staff would simply seek to contain this out-of-control child until his parents arrived, and they would then be invited to take charge. Mysteriously, William always seemed to calm down within a few minutes of his father speaking to him.

Eventually, a staff member overheard William's father's technique for settling his son. He would walk into the room and whisper, "Come on, son, the quicker you settle down the quicker we can get you out of this place." Staff were furious. They felt that William's father was undermining their work and colluding with his son in minimizing the (obviously serious) problem. However, the more they tried to convince the parents of the seriousness of the situation, the more they seemed to dismiss such attempts. The more quickly William seemed to settle for his father, the more difficulty staff had dealing with him at other times.

Exasperated, staff sought advice on how to deal with this situation differently. The conclusion was to take William's father's words at face value rather than seeing them as minimizing. His comment "the quicker you settle down, the quicker we'll be able to get you out of here" could be taken to imply that he believed William was capable of showing self-control and, indeed, capable of behaving well enough to warrant discharge. It was suggested that they acknowledge that William's father obviously knew things about his son that school and unit staff had not recognized. They should discuss with father how he was able to be so sure about his son's ability to control his temper, since this might lead to the discovery of exceptions that could be explored and built upon. Further, whatever the intention of his father's words, it was apparent that William did calm down quickly. Rather than argue the appropriateness of the method, it was more fruitful to seek to highlight its success. In this way, it was possible to engage William's father as an expert who might be able to advise on the management of his son, and to discover examples of control that could be built upon.

The reactions of the staff in this example were understandable. Similarly, the parents' position could be seen to make sense in terms of their view of things. It is not important whether the suggested new explanation of the situation was "true" or not. What matters is that it provided a way for staff and parents to move forward together.

PARENTS ARE PEOPLE, TOO

The fact of the residential treatment situation is that we have the child or adolescent in our program, away from the distractions of the home situation. To some staff, this is the advantage of residential treatment. It is tempting to feel that we can do the real work with these young people without having to deal with parents and others getting in the way.

The other fact is that most of the young people with whom we work will return home. Parents will have to "pick up where we left off." The residential situation is unreal—the unit often has more resources (swimming pool, snooker table, or whatever), the time is extremely focused, and many of the normal realities of life are avoided. To expect parents to continue the same kind of program is unrealistic.

As I have suggested in Chapter 1, the fact of handing over one's child to a residential program is probably one of the most disempowering experiences that there is for a parent. If our aim is to form a cooperative approach to treatment, it is crucial that we validate the experiences of frustration, fear, anguish, and failure that parents have experienced. If they feel that we are acknowledging and validating their experience, they are much more likely to be willing to become involved. I am sure that many instances of parents seeming uncooperative or rejecting are simply reflections of their feeling discounted and blamed.

Validating and respecting the experience of parents is much more than something we might say in a therapy session. It will be reflected in the way we involve them throughout every aspect of the program.

10

TRYING HARD NOT
to WORK TOO HARD:
THE ROLE of STAFF

The residential staff (nurses, youth workers, child-care workers) are an integral part of the residential program. As mentioned previously, the "therapy" conducted in the day-to-day residential activities is often more effective than that conducted in formal therapy sessions.

There is often an expectation that staff will be "in control." However, staff efforts to maintain control sometimes backfire.

We had a 16-year-old boy in our program who had trouble directing his energy into running his life. He was very good at directing his energy into being still. This, however, tricked him into believing he was incapable of doing any of the things he needed to do in order to get on with his life. When things got tough he would sit so still that he couldn't even find the energy to wipe his nose. He came into the unit to learn how to redirect his energy.

After a while, he was having some trouble getting up on time. The staff member on duty discussed it with him and, as a consequence, he was to go to bed a half-hour earlier that night, since his inability to have the energy to get up suggested that he was not getting enough sleep. He refused and was given an extra half-hour the next night and the night after. Finally, I decided that this had gone on long enough and told him to go outside to think about what he was going to do. Again, he refused. I then made a number of mistakes. I had become too in-

volved in his problem and was, therefore, hoping too much for him, instead of allowing him to hope for himself. I also did not take the time to think about what to do. Instead I made the mistake of physically dragging him outside. When I got him outside, he lay on the ground without moving for the next two hours. At least this gave me time to think and to talk to another staff member.

I went back outside and apologized to him for my actions. I then tried to reframe the incident and put it into a different context for him (and for me). I talked about how the problem had tricked us both—him into not directing his energy into his responsibilities and me into taking responsibility for him. I wondered if this was now a chance for him to struggle against the problem and get himself to bed by lights out. I asked him to think about how he could do this. What had he learned in his time in the program about fighting the problem that he could now put into practice? After raising a few questions of this kind, I left him to think about it. One-and-a-half hours later, 15 minutes before lights out, I reminded him of the time but resisted the temptation to ask him what he thought he would do. Just before lights out he managed to get himself up and into bed. He was really struggling with the problem, and it took him about 20 minutes to do this, but what was most important was that he succeeded.

This was a turning point for him. It was the first time he had had such a big victory in his fight against the problem. He learned a lot about his ability to direct his energy and went on in leaps and bounds from there, eventually moving out into a flat of his own.

I also learned a tremendous amount about how my responses to these young people could either get in the way or allow them to struggle with the problem themselves.

—St. Stephen's Youth Accommodation Project,
Adelaide, South Australia

WHOSE RESPONSIBILITY?

Our aim is that the children and adolescents with whom we work will be able to experience themselves as competent and successful. Many people talk about this as "empowering" our clients. It is more than just semantics to say that we cannot ever empower people, for if I do something to empower you, then I must be exercising *my* power to do so. Paradoxically, this must reinforce that I still have more power than you. All we can do is stop doing those things that *disempower* people. They will empower themselves as we provide space for them to discover their ability to do so. This is not a trivial matter, because it highlights the issue of who is responsible for change.

Cade (1989, p. 115) points out that

> It appears that, whenever anyone in a relationship begins, from whatever motivation, to do too much of something, often the other member or members, if they are not moved directly to compete, will tend to start doing less of that something and/or more of an opposite something. . . . Very quickly they can polarize around the issue. The way they polarize seems to say little about their true potentials.
>
> Similarly with responsibility, if one person begins to become over-responsible, it is as though they begin to gather up more than their share of the total responsibility available in the relationship so that the other takes less responsibility, or counters with an opposite such as incompetence or irresponsibility. If you buy a dog and then continue to bark whenever someone knocks on the door, why would the dog do anything more than sleep and eat biscuits? Yet seeing the other's incompetence or irresponsibility becomes the understandable reason for taking on more of the responsibility, and then more of the same leads to more of the same, and so on.

This kind of interactional pattern is often seen in situations where parents and adolescents are embroiled in conflict. Concerned about their son or daughter's well-being and future, parents work harder and harder to encourage, push, or force their adolescent to become more responsible. Of course, if they succeed, then it is they who have taken responsibility for the adolescent's life and all they have usually achieved is compliance. In fact, the adolescent is left in a position of being unable to experience him or herself as having any real opportunity to exercise responsibility or choice.

It seems that, the harder an adult works to bring about change in a child or adolescent, then the less hard the child or adolescent works on changing things. This is not "resistance"—rather, it reflects the fact that the young person does not have the opportunity to see him or herself as having the ability or the responsibility to change.

If parents and their children can become caught in such patterns, then residential staff are even more vulnerable to them. Because our work with children and adolescents is our paid job, we easily feel pressure to make sure that we succeed. My experience suggests that this is usually counterproductive, although challenging our ingrained habits and attitudes is not easy.

"Nagging" Adolescents Is Understandable ...
but Perhaps There Is a Better Way

If we consider the residential placement as a period of transition, an experimental phase, then our aim is that the young people will have the opportunity to "practice" being different. If this is to be meaningful for them and so more likely to lead to sustained change, it is important that they are able to experience their own agency in both success and failure.

This is particularly relevant when we consider the universal tendency adults have to "nag" adolescents, since nagging becomes a way of the adults effectively taking responsibility for successful behavior (that is, if the adolescent is successful, it may be seen as being due to the adult nagging rather than due to the adolescent's own efforts).

> *Matt, age 18, had been struggling with problems of temper outbursts and aggressiveness. He was one of those adolescents who is generally experienced by people as annoying, with the result that people (such as the staff) constantly feel the need to remind, correct, and nag him. Of course, such constant nagging on our part tends to increase his "listening problem," and he seems to hear less and less.*
>
> *We were aware that we were becoming caught in a pattern of trying harder and harder to get Matt to be more responsible and behave differently and that this was counterproductive. Further, we believed that Matt was quite capable of knowing and doing what was required of him, so we discussed a different strategy with him.*
>
> *"Matt, we can see that you are sick of staff talking to you all the time and nagging you to do things. We can see that this drives you crazy and probably doesn't help you do the right things anyway. So we have decided to stop completely reminding you."*
>
> *We explained to Matt that we had made a supply of cards, some red, some yellow, and some green. We explained to him that red meant "Stop immediately," yellow meant "Think about what you are doing," and green signified "Go ahead, do more of what you are doing." Of course, these were exactly the kinds of words we had previously been using to him. We told him that, instead of our telling or nagging him, we would silently give him a card when we noticed him doing something dangerous or unacceptable (red), something perhaps ill-advised (yellow), or something helpful or appropriate (green). He agreed readily to this idea. We mounted a blue card in a pretend glass case in the unit office, marked, "In case of emergency, break glass, and obtain card." If he gave us this card, it would signify that he had urgent need for us to resume directing him and the plan would finish.*

Staff found it difficult to refrain from reminding or nagging Matt; however, the cards helped us do so. As we silently gave Matt the appropriate cards, he was left to take responsibility for his own behavior and make his own choices. Over the ensuing weeks, the number of green cards he received increased. At weekly meetings, the various cards were tallied, and he showed great pride in his growing pile of green. He clearly was beginning to get information about his own behavior in a way that had not been possible when staff were doing all the work.

As Matt became even more happy with a system that offered silent reminders and then left decisions to him, he began to complain that staff were missing opportunities to give him green cards. We apologized, admitting that we had become so used to nagging him about his failings that maybe we were out of practice at noticing his successes. We gave Matt a supply of orange cards. These were "staff reminder cards," and he was to give us an orange card whenever he felt we had not noticed a piece of "green card behavior." These were also tallied at weekly meetings and so provided tangible evidence of our ability to respond to his increasing changes. Importantly, they encouraged him to monitor his own successes, and his behavior was less reliant on our responses.

This card system, which continued for a time before coming naturally to an end, allowed Matt to exercise a greater degree of personal agency in his behavior. More importantly, it forced us to take a step back from our previous position in which we were working harder at changing his behavior than he was.

— Wyatt Lodge, Weldon Centre, Sydney

What was important in this example was not the card system, although it was a helpful way of interrupting the pattern of staff-resident interaction that had developed. Rather, what was important was that staff were prepared to find a way to allow the adolescent to experience himself as controlling and monitoring his own behavior.

Letting Go of Control

Staff are in an extremely difficult position. It is all too easy for them to feel the responsibility for whether things go well or not, and so to feel "defensive" about their own efforts. However, sometimes it is necessary for staff to acknowledge their own invidious position and allow the young person to experience their own degree of control.

Rick was one of those kids who seemed to disobey all the rules. I found myself becoming increasingly frustrated with him and trying more and more ways to establish my control. I felt that I really earned my money while he was in the program, since I had to work hard to try to stay on top of his behavior. One morning, he "freaked out" before school. He and I had been in dispute over his noncompliance, and things escalated to the point where he became completely out-of-control and wouldn't do anything I said. It was a complete stalemate.

After talking to a colleague, I realized that this situation could only escalate further if I did not change tack. Even if, somehow, I managed to regain control, it would have been a very hollow victory. I went back in and apologized to Rick. I apologized for taking too much control, for not letting him experiment with getting himself back in control.

Rick was really shocked. Normally, he would have been asked to apologize for the way he spoke to me (which would often lead to yet another dispute about whether or not he would apologize). My response on this occasion was clearly different for him. His behavior did not "transform," and he did not show a huge reaction (and it was important that I didn't try to elicit one). Nonetheless, it seemed that he was left with something to think about, and things went better afterwards.

— Timaru Hostel, Care Force Youth Services, Sydney

The thought that we must be, and be seen to be, in control is seductive (and the belief that it is possible is probably a delusion). Often, the context of a residential program (expectations of management, colleagues, and parents) promotes a feeling in staff that they must retain control over the behavior of the young people. This easily becomes a situation where staff are trying "to win." However, if they are successful, their victory is often only short-term, and all the residents have learned is that staff are bigger and stronger than they. Of course, if staff set out to win but fail, the implications are even more problematic. If the context is one of a "battle for control," then residents learn that external control and strength is what helps the environment be stable and secure. Not only do staff feel defeated and impotent when they lose, but the young people are likely to experience further insecurity. When young people seem to test the limits even further, this is not usually an attempt to overpower the staff but is an effort to push us to take control. If they have not had the opportunity to experience themselves as having control over their behavior and emotions, then all that is left is to crave external control.

I know residential programs where this kind of altercation would ultimately lead to the resident being restrained by a number of staff, or being given tranquilizing medication forcibly. These "solutions" might restore peace for the moment; however, they do little to help foster a different view of self.

The important thing about the staff member's apology to Rick is not just that it represented a breaking out of the escalating pattern. What is important is that the staff member's comments contained the clear implication that Rick was capable of exercising control over his own behavior. Rick was given the message that staff were no longer going to strive to control his behavior, as well as an expectation that he would do so himself. It was also important that the staff member did not try to elicit a comprehensive reaction from Rick. No single response or intervention will ensure that out-of-control behavior never recurs. In fact, we might expect that Rick would test the staff member's resolve not to take over. However, the interaction has set the stage for things being different and for Rick (and staff) to be more likely to notice and respond to any examples of Rick exercising control over his own behavior.

AHEAD OR BEHIND?

A number of residential staff have found it helpful to think about this balance of responsibility in terms of whether they are taking a position ahead of, or behind, the young person. White (1990, p. 148) suggests that "the therapist's position of supporting persons from behind rather than from ahead is a primary mechanism for the construction of the new receiving context. As a general rule, persons cannot see unique possibilities for their own lives if others are standing in front of them, blocking their view." When we take the position of pushing, encouraging, specifying what needs to be done, and so on—that is, when we take the lead—we place ourselves ahead of the young person, who is left with little option other than to try to catch up to us (or, alternatively, to give up). If he or she is successful, little more has been achieved than meeting *our* expectations and *our* goals, and there is little room for feeling any real accomplishment. If, on the other hand, we hold fast to the view that our clients are capable of change, and capable of knowing what will work best for them, then we will remain behind the young person. It will be clear that it is he or she who is making the moves and that our job is to recognize these and "catch up" to what is being achieved. Not only does this position allow the young person to feel a greater degree of personal agency in what is achieved, but it also helps staff focus more on identifying examples of success.

Vanessa, age 17, had been in our long-term unit for more than a year. She had been a victim of sexual assault, and the behavior that prompted her admission included heavy drug and alcohol use, suicidal thoughts and actions, and periods of prostitution. This behavior had continued during her time in our unit.

We were acutely aware of our responsibility for her safety and so we monitored her drug use carefully. As her behavior became more dangerous, we imposed stricter curfews, did not allow her to be on her own without supervision, scrutinized any parcels she brought into the unit, and so on. On occasion, she would go out, and then later phone us, obviously stoned and wanting us to pick her up, but she would not tell us where she was. It was easy to spend hours searching for her.

The more we did to take responsibility for her safety, the more unsafe her behavior became. We realized that we were doing all the work and, inadvertently, were depriving Vanessa of the opportunity to experience herself as having any control over her situation. This finally became clear to us one day when Vanessa was extremely "down." She drew a picture representing her situation: a large merry-go-round, which she said was spinning faster and faster. She was on the merry-go-round, unable to stop it, and no one else could get close to it because of a barbed-wire fence. She drew us (the staff) outside the fence with a bullhorn, shouting directions to her. In the center of the merry-go-round was a "stop" button. This was the first indication we had that Vanessa had any belief that the merry-go-round could stop (although we suspected that our attempts to scramble over the fence to the stop button had probably just pushed the merry-go-round to spin faster).

We asked Vanessa about the stop button, wondering how close she had been able to get to it and what she imagined pressing it would be like. We also told her that we realized it was not very helpful for us to shout instructions to her from afar and apologized that we had been doing so. Since she was the closest to the button, she didn't need our direction about reaching it. In fact, we suggested that Vanessa ought to have the bullhorn so she could tell us what she should do, rather than ask our advice.

We resolved that we would give back control of the situation to Vanessa. This was a struggle, both for us and for her. We found it difficult given our awareness of the risks, and Vanessa had not really had the chance before to experiment with being in control. When Vanessa was going out, we would ask her questions about how she knew she would be safe and ask her if she had the bullhorn. Not surprisingly, there were occasions when Vanessa was not able to keep things under control; however, she "had the bullhorn" and chose to ask us for help. As she continued to struggle, she became more able to appreciate her successes. Previously, if we tried to point out small steps or excep-

*tions to Vanessa, she found it hard to acknowledge them. Now that she
sees herself more in control of things, she is telling us herself about her
successes.*

*Vanessa's struggle has taken a great deal of courage. We realize that
previously the courage and strength was ours, whereas now Vanessa
has had space to discover her own courage and strength.*

— *Wyatt Lodge, Weldon Centre, Sydney*

When there are issues of safety involved, it is difficult for residential
staff to let go of ideas that they must maintain control. There are justifi-
able concerns about staff's "duty of care," legal implications if staff are seen
to have been negligent, and concerns about criticism from supervisors.
Nonetheless, it seems that working harder and harder to keep young people out of trouble *just does not work.*

I remember a residential child-psychiatry unit in which I worked, where
the director removed all the locks on doors and gates. His rationale was
that "Locks don't slow the kids down at all, they just make life more
difficult for the staff!" We might add to this explanation the fact that it
does not help young people develop a different view of themselves simply
by learning that locks are seen as necessary to control them.

We face a continual balance between the demands of our professional
responsibilities and the risks that are involved in allowing young people to
experiment with self-control. Placing ourselves ahead of the young people
is safer. Staying behind can be unsettling and risky and requires an organizational environment that supports staff taking calculated risks. In the
long run, it often works better.

The senior worker in one residential program had worked hard on finding ways to stay behind the residents. Despite expectations that he, as
senior worker, would step in when things got out of hand, he realized that
to do so ran the risk both of depriving the young people opportunities to
experience being in control, and also of undermining the other staff. He
saw his role as one of helping staff review their responses and discuss ways
that they might become caught up in working too hard, and he worked
hard on not working too hard himself. One day, a resident asked him,
"Are you a casual staff person, or a relief worker?" To him, this was evidence that he was managing to maintain his "behind" position.

REFLECTIONS ON NOT WORKING TOO HARD

As part of my preparation of this book, I discussed with a group of
youth workers their experiences of using the types of ideas outlined in the

book and of working hard on not working too hard. They are the youth work team in a medium to long-term residential unit for older adolescent boys (15 to 18 years old), many of whom have had previous placements and involvement with the police and courts. Many have histories including violence to people or property. The program has a definite therapeutic focus, although it also includes living-skills training and practical aspects such as looking for work.

Michael: What kinds of differences have using these ideas made to you?

Martin: One difference this way of working makes is that it tends to ask you to stop and think about things, it encourages you to look at things like the meaning of the situation for the particular kid and the interactional things in the unit. Having that whole idea of slowing down and thinking about what you do.

Campbell: Just to have a framework at all, a way of working that the whole team works on, is quite different to some other places I've worked.

Jan: We work as a team, so we all have the same responses, which is very different to the experiences the kids have had at home.

Martin: It's interesting how often we hear a kid say something like, "You all always say the same thing"—we're all thinking along the same lines and coming up with similar kinds of solutions.

Campbell: We train ourselves to respond rather than react to the residents' behavior, which means we have to think before we do anything.

Ewan: If you try to deal with things straight away, you often end up reacting rather than responding. However if you stop and think, or maybe take some time to talk to someone else, you can give a much clearer, more appropriate message.

Jan: Yes, and it also helps not to get caught up in ideas of their intent. It's easy to start thinking that they are intentionally disrupting the house, which isn't helpful.

Michael: Okay, so it's fine to talk about stopping and thinking, but don't you have a responsibility to have some control over things?

Ewan: Taking responsibility for them is easy while they're here, but it doesn't help them when they get out into the world.

Jan: I see my role as giving them as much information as possible to make a choice, but which choice they make is not my responsibility.

Campbell: Part of the context of the house is that we're prepared to let them experiment with both sorts of behavior—acceptable and unacceptable, and there's information that comes from both. If the behavior is unacceptable, the consequence aims to give them some new information. If we can highlight when their behavior is acceptable, that helps them begin to see themselves as being in control.

Michael: What do you mean by "experiment"?

Campbell: I guess we don't see that the house has to run as a perfect unit all the time, and there can be times when things seem out of control, but we are prepared to experiment with giving the residents as much time as possible to get things back under control rather than us stepping in to get the house running smoothly.

Gillian: It comes down to giving as many chances for success as possible.

Michael: Aren't they chances for failure as well?

Gillian: I guess so, but only if it ends there.

Campbell: They're more likely to get a message of failure if somebody else steps in than if they ultimately, even after a long struggle, manage to take some control themselves.

Martin: Yes, if we step in, that leaves them feeling "I couldn't do it myself."

Jan: To me, stepping in is such a short-term solution because the more you step in, the more the kid is going to need someone to step in and the less it prepares them for the future. We need to give them the chance slowly to build up control and notice the difference between being in control and being out of control. By letting them struggle, it might give them the chance to take some control but it also can give the message that to fail once isn't the end of the line. Many of them have come from places where they are just controlled for a long time, and the control just becomes stronger and stronger. If they only ever experience someone else controlling their behavior then that's what they will keep needing, and they are more likely to end up in the security system for the rest of their lives. We hope they might experience a different option — of being able to control themselves.

Campbell: In this place, they're not locked in, and they have quite a deal of freedom. Because the workers are not continually trying to take control and set too high expectations for the residents, it is more feasible that they can operate reasonably in this environment and progress. We had a worker join our staff who had worked previously in a more structured, controlling institution. He was surprised to find a resident in our program who had also been in the same institution previously, and he commented on how much calmer this young person was in this situation than he had been in the institutional setting where staff worked hard to keep him calm. I think the degree of relative freedom we have actually gives the residents the opportunity to experiment with being responsible for themselves in ways that a more restrictive situation doesn't.

Jan: It is hard when something's going on in the house, and you know that the most helpful thing is to sit back and let it take its course and deal with it afterwards. You feel like "I should do something," and it's hard just to sit on your hands.

Campbell: The turning point for me was when I realized that how the place is running is the residents' responsibility and not mine. My responsibility is to give them opportunities to experience being responsible and continually to notice things they do differently, not to make sure that the place runs smoothly all the time.

Jan: That doesn't mean we just sit in the office and let chaos reign around us. But I often realize that the reaction that first comes to mind is often not helpful in helping the young people feel like they can change things in their lives. So sitting back, waiting and thinking allows me to make a choice about when and how to intervene. I can think about whether the best thing is to ask a question to invite the resident to think about his behavior, or highlight some positive aspect of the behavior, or impose some sort of consequence for the negative behavior. Taking time works better.

Campbell: Yes, we certainly don't just sit back and do nothing. And it can be a trap for us to feel like we've always got to come up with some clever way of responding that stops the behavior and that if it doesn't stop then we've failed. It isn't helpful to put that kind of pressure on ourselves. Sometimes you could have a hundred clever interventions but the behavior doesn't stop. And sometimes we just have to say, "No, that's not on" and be really firm and deal with the resulting uproar.

Jan: Lots of the kids don't really think they have choices. Even when we have to set limits and stick to them, the residents still experience the choice of having control over their own reactions.

Ewan: Yes, even some kids who have left apparently unsuccessfully, when we've followed them up later, we discover that the opportunities they had to experience choices, even the ones that did not seem to work, have made a difference.

Do We Serve the Program or Does the Program Serve Us?

All residential programs have administrative and organizational requirements. Added to these are the requirements of funding bodies, government welfare or health departments, and so on. These requirements often include specifications for record-keeping, statistics, regular case reviews, and so on. Here in Sydney, out-of-home placements are usually supervised to some extent by the state welfare authorities, who impose detailed requirements concerning case planning, reporting, and formal case conferences. Of course, such accountability and the need to have some planning and review in our work is important, but it sometimes reaches a point where we can begin to wonder whose needs it is that we are meeting.

When we are working with troubled, or troubling, young people, there are other prescriptions for us and our programs apart from these "formal" requirements. By the time a young person comes to a residential program, he or she has often been involved with a number of professionals, many of whom will have ideas about the kinds of treatment that are required. Young people often come to our programs with large files or detailed referral information, which may include opinions about particular kinds of therapy or management that are required.

How do we balance all these competing demands? Certainly, it can sometimes feel like we are serving the system rather than the system being something that helps us work most effectively with young people and their families.

It is important that we distinguish between the role of therapy and the role of social control. In the welfare field, these are often blurred or confused, yet they are distinct activities. Social control endeavors that seek to ensure a person's safety, for example, are often valid, and we may seek to carry them out in as "therapeutic" a way as possible; nonetheless, they are not treatment. In social control activities, it is clear that the professionals or the authorities are the ones with the power and the expertise. In therapeutic concerns, our aim is that clients will experience themselves as having the solution to their difficulties. This focus will sometimes entail taking risks, allowing clients space to experiment and perhaps to fail.

One residential program decided to refuse to allow the court to commit young people to it. Rather, they agreed that they were happy to work with court-ordered young people but specified that these young people should be ordered by the court to the care of the local Welfare Department director and not to the program. In many ways, this made little difference in what happened day-to-day. However, it made a couple of important differences in terms of the overall process. First, it meant that someone else was responsible for the "statutory" requirements, making it easier for these not to compromise the program's ability to provide a context of experimentation. Second, it allowed greater flexibility about admission and discharge, since leaving the program or changing the treatment plan did not require a new court order.

The way we approach the various prescriptions that external agencies impose upon us is again primarily a matter of the way we think about our task. Most of the procedures that are required of us can be implemented in ways that potentially disempower our clients, or can be framed in ways that make them part of the ongoing process of developing views of competence.

Our agency has previously had a policy of regular case reviews for each child in the program. These have often also been necessary to meet the state welfare department requirements and have usually involved agency staff, welfare department staff, and any other significant professionals involved. These reviews have usually involved reviewing the goals for the child and setting future goals for the case plan.

We realized that some of our residents were hesitant about attending these meetings or about contributing to the goal-setting. Of course, it was easy to interpret this hesitancy as their unwillingness to be involved or their inability to examine their own case plans, with the result that a majority of the adults present would often determine the plan.

After further thought we recognized that, for many of the young people, case reviews were just one more thing that was being "done to them." Whether the adults present expressed excitement about the young person's progress or devised yet another list of goals (which is often what seems to happen at such meetings), the young person was not really part of this and was left having to "catch up" to the adults.

We decided not to have these case reviews any more. Instead, we instituted "catch up meetings"—meetings at which the young person could help us "catch up" with where he or she was. We invited the resident to set the dates (perhaps from a list of suggested dates given by us) and to decide who should be invited. In this way, the meetings do not represent that group considered by "the system" to be relevant, but the people whom the young person thinks should be aware of what's happening. This makes it much more realistic for us to talk about the young person having his or her own agenda, with us simply providing a safe environment where he or she can experiment.

Since making this change, we have realized that there are other ways that what we "know best" may actually be imposed upon the young people in a way that leaves them behind, trying to catch up with us.

Nathan came to our unit with the agenda that he needed to work on issues connected with his sexual abuse. Previous placements had been less than successful and the various workers, all with Nathan's interests at heart, had decided that his treatment had neglected important issues. Accordingly, the prescription with which he came was that he should have therapy that would help him "work through" his sexual abuse.

Nathan protested that he did not want therapy. He acknowledged that he might want counseling at some stage, but was not yet ready for it. It would have been easy for us to interpret this as evidence of defensiveness or denial and so feel even more strongly that therapy was indicated. However, we were aware that a "keeping behind" position required that we credit Nathan with the ability to determine what was best for him. Accordingly, we agreed that he could exercise his own options about what would be helpful. If he chose to "work on" nothing, that was okay with us—as long as he met the various house expectations of conduct, etc. It was hard for us to sit back and watch Nathan appearing to be doing little more than "boarding," since we had always thought that a good placement involved a specific therapeutic agenda—something to work on. Nonetheless, we made ourselves stick to our resolve not to get "in front" of Nathan.

After a while, Nathan became more amenable to talking about his agenda. He was quite clear that he was afraid of his temper getting out of control, therefore he made sure that he did not react to anything, and hence spent his time feeling enormous internal pressure. This was meaningful for him, and something he wanted to address; however, other peoples' attempts to set the therapeutic agenda had left him feeling unable to meet their expectations and unable to express his own concerns. As we accepted Nathan's agenda and provided space where he could experiment with getting angry, he has gradually been able to speak up and see himself as more in control of his own emotions.

Recently, Nathan asked us if he could move on to the Independent Living Skills phase of our program. We discussed with him the fact that the normal requirement for moving to the next phase is that the young person is doing all his required tasks in the unit and that Nathan had not been doing his. He pointed out to us, "If I have to do things for myself, I'm more likely to do them rather than when I have to do them for other people." Again, a lesson in "staying behind." Our criterion for moving on easily became a hurdle that Nathan had to face, with the result that it would be harder for him to appreciate his own efforts in achieving it. Allowing Nathan to move ahead when he felt ready (with some discussion about what made him think he was ready) left him in the position of being able to experience his own agency—both in his success and his failure. In fact, Nathan's success in the next phase of the program, and his willingness to seek our advice, left us well and truly behind and needing to catch up to him.

—Wyatt Lodge, Weldon Centre, Sydney

ANOTHER (EXTREME) EXAMPLE OF
"LETTING GO" OF CONTROL

From time to time, we would ask residents to devise their own consequences for infractions of the house expectations. Often, we would frame this as, "I realize I've been working harder than you at trying to change your behavior, and I need a break. It wears me out and probably just gets you feeling even more mad. So, you need to work out what consequence fits for you here."

This fit with our continual efforts to give back responsibility to the young people as much as possible. It meant that things did not always go the way we expected, yet we felt that allowing them to experience personal responsibility was far more useful than anything we might say about being responsible.

Letting go of our need to be in control was sometimes a challenge. For example, there was one occasion when a new resident was coming to spend just one night in the house as part of the process of deciding if this was where he wished to stay for a while. The group of residents we had was fairly stable, and they complained loudly about the disruption caused by this "intruder." Their complaints continued and attempts to get them to "be reasonable" were useless. At our weekly house meeting, we framed the incident as having been our fault in that we had not notified the residents beforehand that this young person would be visiting, and so they had not had the opportunity to prepare themselves for having an outsider in the house. In this way, we hoped that we might defuse the idea that it was the visitor's behavior that had upset them (leaving them better able to get on with him if he did eventually move into the unit). This was not completely a tactical move. We felt that our failure to prepare them probably had contributed to the disruption.

The unexpected part of this was that one of the young people suggested that the staff should have consequences for their irresponsible behavior. Before we had time to think of a clever response, the other residents joined in. Since the staff had disrupted the smooth running of the unit, they said, we should have the consequence of carrying out all the residents' domestic chores for a week. "How does that consequence connect with our forgetfulness?" we asked. "Because if you have to do our chores, you'll never forget again to tell us things!"

We carried out the chores for the next week without complaining, and the residents delighted in ensuring that we did so. We felt that this episode provided a number of opportunities for discussing their thinking about behavior and its consequences, and for showing that we were not simply there to be in control.

Next time we had a short-term admission, we made sure that we told the current residents about it. We also delivered notes, placed under each of their doors, just to be sure.

— Trigg Hostel, Care Force Youth Services, Sydney

SCHEDULING STAFF TO PREVENT BURN-OUT

Every aspect of the program will either facilitate a climate that encourages self-control and experimentation or will make it more likely that staff will assume a degree of responsibility or control and that will ensure that real experimentation is impossible. Even such things as staff rosters are important in this regard.

In some "group home" style programs in Australia, residential staff often work a number of 24-hour shifts in a row. Sometimes, this arrangement includes the notion that they work during the day and then simply "sleep over" and are unlikely to have to work during the night. I sometimes think such rosters were designed by people who have never experienced the nocturnal activities of most children and adolescents! In some cases, this kind of roster has developed from a former situation where a unit was staffed by "house parents," who actually lived there and were always on duty. In others, it seems to reflect an idea that having staff present for a number of days and nights in a row will promote consistency and help the children build secure relationships. In many programs, I suspect that this kind of arrangement is primarily the result of budgetary constraints. Often, in my experience, the staff themselves are happy with such an arrangement since they enjoy the four or more days off they have at the end of each period of duty.

However, what context is fostered by this kind of staffing arrangement? When spending 24 hours or more with a group of children or adolescents, staff are much more likely to fall into the same kinds of patterns in which parents find themselves. The situation is such that they are much more likely to think of themselves as "caregivers" than as "professionals." If our aim is that every aspect of the program should further our therapeutic aims, we need to ensure that our staff have the time and space to think about their responses and act in a purposeful manner. As a therapist, I would not consider scheduling clients for 15 consecutive hours. Sometimes, even after less time than that, I am so drained (even if I do not feel physically tired) that my responses to my clients become reactions rather than responses. That is, I do or say something in reply to the most recent event without considering its part in the entire therapeutic process. I believe that the most important residential therapy is done by the day-to-day residential staff. However, it is unrealistic to expect them to be effective if they are spending so many hours with the residents.

I should stress that I have seen many programs where residential staff work such long hours faithfully and in ways that provide a secure and helpful environment for the children or adolescents with whom they are working. Nonetheless, I have more often seen staff in this situation become caught up in escalating patterns of interaction with residents, slip back into feeling personally threatened by apparent loss of control, and lose their "objectivity." Many of the examples and suggestions mentioned earlier in this chapter of staff "working hard on not working hard," and many of the examples in Chapter 8 about approaches to discipline that sought not just to take control of a situation, would be difficult to expect from staff who have the pressure of the normal demands of residents over a prolonged period.

Rotating eight-hour shifts (or similar arrangements) require more staff and are thus more costly. Twenty-four hour shifts may ultimately be more costly in terms of staff burnout and reduced effectiveness.

RESIDENTIAL PROGRAMS SHOULD NOT BE CHILD-CENTERED

This statement may seem to be at variance with everything else in this book, but it is not.

I have suggested a number of times that our program should be oriented towards therapeutic aims. Our concern is that the children and adolescents (and their families) should develop new views of themselves. To this extent, we must be child-focused in our work.

Nonetheless, as I suggested in the previous section, my observation is that the most "therapeutic" work is often carried out by the residential staff rather than by designated therapists. That is, the most effective "clinicians" are usually the staff who are lowest in the administrative and professional hierarchy (and usually paid less). I have met residential staff—youth workers, child-care workers, and nurses—in various parts of the world, who feel undervalued and unsupported. They feel a responsibility to ensure that things run smoothly, but only receive comments from management when something is going wrong!

My hope is that the ideas and examples in this book will offer some helpful ways for program managers, therapy staff, and residential staff to work with young people and families. However, I believe the single, most important variable in the effectiveness of residential programs is the extent to which the "frontline" staff experience themselves as valued and supported. Too many agencies put too much work into focusing on the children and adolescents at the expense of directing resources towards staff.

I have had a number of experiences of being asked to consult to agencies about particular children or adolescents with whom they were experiencing difficulties. Often, these situations had reached crisis point, with the feeling that a resident might have to be asked to leave. I would be asked to help devise a program for the particular child or adolescent or offer some "outside" perspective on how staff might manage the situation. In many such situations, I find myself faced with residential staff who have borne the brunt of prolonged difficulties and who feel defeated and powerless. Feeling this way, they are quite likely to be skeptical about any suggestions offered. To "impose" another program is to introduce another possibility for them to feel undermined and powerless. Often, my sense is that what is required is not that a child or adolescent be moved, and not that a new program be introduced. Rather, what is required is that the staff be given more tangible support and that such support be offered in ways that do not imply that something is being done to "rectify" a situation that has got out of hand.

> *Our residential program involved a team of therapists and a number of different units. One unit was on the same campus as the therapists' offices, the others were varying distances away (the furthest being nearly a two-hour drive). A few years ago, we went through a period of having enormous difficulties with one of the units. The youth work staff seemed intent on undermining our therapeutic plans. They devised excuses for having not followed through with our suggestions or case plans. They seemed to have less and less control over the running of the unit, and the residents were frequently out-of-control. We came to the conclusion that staff were either incompetent or deliberately oppositional.*
>
> *Concerned about this situation, we sought to offer further advice and training, to make even clearer our expectations with regard to specific case plans, and we found ourselves checking and rechecking their understanding of these plans. We wanted to support them, so were quick to respond whenever the staff experienced difficulty with a resident. Unfortunately, all this seemed to no avail, and the situation continued to deteriorate, to the point that we became concerned about admitting adolescents to the unit.*

When I have recounted this story in the past, people have tried to guess which unit was the one with the difficulties. Some predict it was the unit furthest away, since the staff there were most likely to feel unsupported.

In fact, it was the unit that was on site. To understand this, we need to think about the way the situation itself promoted a broader context that worked against the staff of this unit seeing themselves, and so behaving, as competent.

> *Finally, we realized we needed to look at the broader context of this "problem." We realized that there were significant differences between how we related to the unit that was on site compared to the units that were further away. When a youth worker from the unit two hours away phoned one of the therapists to say, "Your adolescent is out of control, what are you going to do about it?" the therapist was likely to reply, "Okay, I can be there next Tuesday." Of course, by the time next Tuesday arrived, the staff had already (out of necessity) dealt with the situation. That meant that our discussion focused on how they had been able to settle the situation down—that is, we discussed their success. However, when staff from the unit on site telephoned (or shouted from the window) about a "crisis," the therapist concerned would rush to their assistance and take over the situation. This meant that they never had the opportunity to experience themselves as being successful. Therefore, they felt less and less competent, therapists responded to apparent crises more and more quickly, and the staff were undermined more and more. Once a situation was over, all that was left to discuss was how the staff had been unsuccessful. Both they and the residents began to expect therapy staff to intervene, and became accordingly less and less confident. When things reached the point where the residents themselves were the ones shouting for therapist assistance, we realized something was wrong!*

The therapists, of course, had the best of intentions. Common sense said that they should help the staff who were finding things hard going. However, the therapists were inadvertently becoming caught in the same pattern of "working too hard" as we have seen may happen between staff and residents. In this situation, the more responsibility the therapists took for trying to solve the situation, the less their residential colleagues were able to experience themselves as having any responsibility or efficacy. This is not to say that therapy (or other) staff should not support residential staff—such support is crucial. However, we need continually to remind ourselves that everything we do happens within a particular meaning-context. If we wish to offer support and encouragement to residential staff, we need to do so from a consideration of how they are experiencing the particular situation. Otherwise, we may easily become caught in "more of the same" patterns.

In such situations, we need also to consider other factors that contribute to the overall context.

On further examination, we realized that the situation was compounded by a number of (apparently quite sensible) administrative procedures. For example, each unit had its own petty cash fund, for use in taking residents on outings, etc. In most units, the senior worker could authorize certain expenditures and was then required to account for them. However, given that this unit was on the same site as the therapy team's offices, management had decided it made sense to have a single petty cash fund. This meant that youth workers had to request money from the therapy team's secretary when they needed it. To make matters worse, the therapists all had keys to the residential unit and could (and would) walk in unannounced whenever they needed to talk to staff. This was in marked contrast to the other units, since practical considerations meant that therapists would need to make an appointment to visit. There were even more apparently minor matters that contributed to this situation of blurred boundaries. For example, if a therapist was suffering a headache, it was easy to walk into the unit and use the unit's supply of analgesics. Of course, residential staff experienced this as yet another example of the therapists' arrogance.

It was not until we acknowledged that we had been acting in ways that left staff experiencing themselves as powerless and incompetent that we had a way to deal with this impasse.

—Care Force Youth Services, Sydney

RESPONDING TO STAFF SUCCESS

Since our approach is not one of finding "fancy therapeutic techniques," but of harnessing the resources that already exist (but may be unnoticed), we might adopt similar strategies in our support of staff. Residential staff, as I have experienced them, are largely committed, dedicated, and energetic. We ought to take these aspects seriously in the way we manage and supervise residential staff. Encouraging staff to build upon what they are doing that is helpful is likely to be more useful than trying to "reform" their way of thinking.

In writing a solution-oriented program for an inpatient hospital I learned that changing the philosophy of problem-oriented staff can be quite difficult. The staff were caught up in discovering the "roots" of the problems yet were often unsuccessful and frustrated with the results.

As their philosophy began to change into a greater focus on solutions, they often seemed to think that they needed to do more. However, the proof in patient changes helped convince them that "less was more."

I encouraged staff members to set weekly personal goals for their own roles based on what had worked best the previous week. We made a chart, which hung in the staff meeting room, and which encouraged the staff member and his or her peers to note personal goals and achievements and "exceptional work this week" (Figure 10.1).

Of course, this was a way of encouraging staff to participate in virtually the same kind of process as their patients, and they seemed to adopt this idea and become more naturally oriented to responding to those things their colleagues were doing that were helpful. This took some time and the Program Director needed to attend to the chart and encourage the staff to complete it. Over time, we found that staff looked forward to the review of the chart, which was part of the weekly staff meeting, and that they injected a degree of humour into the process.

— Linda Metcalf, Arlington, Texas

Name	"Exceptional work this week"	Goals
	(comments written by peers during the week as well as by the staff member concerned)	(where the staff member wants to be next week at this time—described in specific, behavioral terms, in relation to particular patients; this encourages peers to notice times when the staff member achieves this goal)

FIGURE 10.1:   A Chart to Help Staff Members Respond to Their Own Successes

11

WHERE DOES
"THERAPY" FIT IN?

I have already suggested that it is the entire context of the residential program that may be seen as "the therapy," rather than just some activity that occurs in a designated therapy room. I well remember, when I worked in an inpatient child and adolescent psychiatry unit, my growing suspicion that what I did in the "therapy room" (with comfortable chairs, video camera, and one-way mirror) was ultimately not nearly as effective as the "therapeutic" interactions that occurred around the pool table, the trampoline, and the dining room. The kinds of programs described throughout this book rely less and less on formal therapy and more and more on an integrated process that utilizes every aspect of the day-to-day to allow young people and families to discover and build upon strengths and competencies.

In fact, I know of a number of programs that include no explicit therapy component. In particular, there are a number of programs in Australia that are, officially, youth accommodation or "youth refuge" programs. They were established without any recognition of a therapeutic focus. Of course, staff have discovered that most of the young people who come to their programs have difficulties beyond simply that of homelessness, and so have adopted a more therapeutic stance. Since they have not been funded to employ therapists, such programs have been forced to find ways to include "therapy" in the day-to-day program and have often found that both the young people and their parents respond more readily to this than they would to designated "therapy sessions." The activities of the program

159

and the responses of staff, following the theme established for the placement, provide a framework within which discoveries are made without
the need for formal therapy sessions. These programs rely heavily on different ways of involving parents such as those described in the Chapter 9.

Nonetheless, many residential programs do include some form of family, group, and/or individual therapy as part of the process. However,
therapy is thought of a little differently than usual. It is not seen as a way
to "intervene" or to "solve the families' problems." Rather, it is a forum for
involvement in planning and decision-making and for information sharing
and highlighting. If our aim is that the young person will return home,
the likelihood of this happening successfully depends on parents feeling
involved in the process. Therapy sessions offer an opportunity for enhancing this sense of involvement.

WHERE ARE DECISIONS MADE? (HOW WE THINK ABOUT "FAMILY THERAPY")

A rule-of-thumb adopted by a number of programs is that **no** decision is
made about a child or adolescent's program except in a meeting or family
therapy session with his or her parents.

Often, in the past, decisions about the treatment program were made
by the professional staff, and parents were informed when it was conve-
nient. After all, they had signed consent forms and, in effect, had handed
over responsibility to the program and the staff. In many ways, this is
more efficient and easier. The problem is that it easily contributes to the
continued alienation of parents, making it more likely that they will either
do things that staff see as "undermining" the program or will approach
their child's discharge with a sense of skepticism as they look for evidence
that the experts' techniques have not worked.

A cooperative approach is essential in ensuring that parents are part of
the process and are "on our side." As such, it is not enough that they
appear to be involved—rather, they need to feel that they are an integral
part of the "team." As was highlighted in Chapter 9, this is not just a
stance we adopt as part of pursuing our therapeutic ends. Parents do have
resources and skills, they are experts concerning their own child, and we
ignore them at our peril. One example in Chapter 9 described a program
where parents were consulted frequently to make decisions about discipline and so on. This approach might not fit every situation; however, it is
almost always possible to involve parents in the major decisions about
the program—deciding on particular activities, negotiating changes in the
program, and so on.

Thus, an important aspect of therapy sessions that occur during the
admission is that they become essentially "team meetings," where parents

and young person are treated as equal (but different) members of the treatment team.

Many staff will raise questions or complaints about this suggestion: "What about those parents who are not prepared to be involved?" and "But treatment decisions often have to be made in a hurry, we cannot wait until the next session!" As I suggested in the first chapter, parents' apparent unwillingness to be involved often is a reflection of their sense of failure and hopelessness and the extent to which they may have been "trained" into incompetence, apathy, and antagonism by a succession of previous workers. Often, once parents realize that staff are not seeking to blame them and are actually treating them as people with skills and competence, they become more willing to be involved. This may take some time, and different parents will be happy with different degrees of involvement. However, staff need continually to operate from the view that parents are part of the therapy team and conduct family therapy sessions in a way that reflects this. As far as "crises" and "immediate decisions" are concerned, we ought carefully to examine how we view such situations. Many therapists come to learn that there are few "crises" that absolutely cannot wait—and faced in "the cool light of day," some time later, solutions are often more readily discovered. As much as possible, staff should avoid making major decisions without consulting the young person and family in a family session or meeting. Of course, this could tend to become a bit like the "wait until your father gets home!" stance of some parents, and it is not meant to be. It is only likely to become viewed in this way if it is a "technique" grafted onto an otherwise staff-dominated program rather than being a natural outworking of the general "climate" of the program. When a situation requires staff to make major decisions unilaterally, they should aim to discuss these with the family and should genuinely seek their comments as soon as possible afterwards.

The stance reflected in this suggestion is inevitably more difficult. It is much easier for staff to retain control over the program and the decisions involved. However, such a view is short-sighted, since it usually proves not to be easier in the longer term. Regarding family therapy sessions not as a time when we professionals "work on" the problems of the family, but as an opportunity for mutual consultation and decision-making, will usually contribute to more harmonious and more effective treatment.

SHARING INFORMATION ABOUT SUCCESS

The second important function of family therapy sessions within this approach is as a forum for sharing information about success. Again, our aim is that the process be as cooperative and as competency-based as possible. Therefore, we may think of therapy sessions as a forum for exchanging information rather than as something we professionals do to our clients.

I have suggested that one of the major things that contributes to the persistence of problems is people's inability (due to their constructs or view of things) to notice difference or success. As long as people notice only "problem behaviors" then those are the only behaviors to which they can respond and, as they continue to respond to these, patterns of problem interaction continue. Change does not just (or primarily) require that people *do* something different, it requires that they be able to notice and respond to solution behavior.

As the period of "transition" proceeds, staff will be looking out for any signs of success or difference in the young person's behavior and seeking to respond to these. A number of residential staff have commented to me that, despite the fact that they began this process somewhat skeptically and seeing it as little more than their "therapeutic task," the concentration on exceptions or successes actually led to them beginning to think differently about the residents. Similarly, parents and other family members can come to think differently about the child or adolescent, however they do not have the same day-to-day opportunities to notice small changes.

Family therapy sessions, then, become an important opportunity for sharing information with parents about the young person's progress. Just as, when responding to the young person, it is often not helpful for staff to become too excited about progress, so it is often not helpful to present parents with a list of the week's successes. This may become an invitation for them (from their prevailing view of the situation) to "discount" these steps. Rather, it is preferable to report various achievements as matter-of-factly as possible and ask parents if they are able to explain these apparent changes. They might be asked to speculate on what difference these kinds of changes will make when they continue, or how they think they might find themselves responding differently when these things happen in the home situation.

It is easy for parents to feel that therapists are trying to convince them that their son or daughter is improving. After all, that is their job. Therefore, the most useful people to provide information in therapy sessions are the youth work, child-care, or residential staff. They live with the residents and are able more genuinely to share the frustrations they experience, which is important in validating the experiences parents have had in the past. From this position, residential staff are then better able to share information about successes and change. Since we see therapy sessions as a cooperative exchange of information, rather than as "interventions," and since the most important information to share will include the resident's day-to-day progress, I believe it is imperative that a residential worker always be included in the sessions.

REVIEWING PARENTS' PRACTICE

It is the child or adolescent who is in the residential program, but, as described earlier, the theme for the placement will often include some "practice" on the part of the parents. This might take the form of particular tasks parents are undertaking (such as the father who was taking various practical steps to prepare to parent his teenage daughters — "Becoming a family slowly" in Chapter 3), particular consideration of how they might respond differently to problem behavior (such as the parents who became "growing up coaches" — as described in "A celebration" in the next chapter), or parents using their son or daughter's visits home to practice different strategies (as in the mother who was practicing letting her son take grater responsibility in the "Having good days" example in Chapter 4).

These things are important in helping the residential program be one that involves the entire family, and so reducing the focus on "the identified patient." However, they are wasted if the work with parents happens separately from that with the child or adolescent. Not only must the family be involved in the process, but also it must be *seen* to be involved (particularly by the young person). Hence, family therapy sessions become an opportunity not only for parents to receive information about their son or daughter's progress but also for the young person to receive information about his or her parents' progress.

This can be an important part of the resident not feeling like it is just him or her who is receiving treatment and so can make a great difference to how the family, and the possibility of returning home, is viewed by all involved. After discussing the successes of the young person, as described above, therapy sessions can review the achievements of parents and the gains they have made. As much as possible, these discussions should focus on actual events where parents thought or behaved differently. Since our focus is on success rather than failure (or "issues"), the process need not be threatening to parents and can help reestablish the bond between parent and child.

WHICH MODEL OF THERAPY?

This chapter has considered the place of family therapy within the residential program, however I have deliberately *not* discussed any specific approach to, or "model" of, therapy.

The focus of this book is on the overall "climate" of the residential unit — the process of building an overall milieu that enhances competence. Within that task, various different approaches to therapy might be employed. Different therapists in different programs have their preferred approaches and preferred styles. My own preference is for a "solution-focused" approach, as reflected in the work of de Shazer and his colleagues (de Shazer, 1988, 1991) and as adapted by others in different contexts (Durrant & Kowalski, 1993; Furman & Ahola, 1992; O'Hanlon & Weiner-Davis, 1989; Walter & Peller, 1992). This approach derives from an orientation that is explicitly focused on "what is going right" or "what may be built on," and so is immediately consistent with the assumptions that underlie this discussion of residential work. Other approaches may be equally useful. What is important is not the specific therapeutic techniques or methods, but their overall focus.

HOW MUCH THERAPY? WHAT SORT OF THERAPY?

There is a wide variety in types of residential programs, and they include various structured therapy activities to varying degrees. I know a number of programs, particularly those that operate within the nongovernment, charitable sector, that involve weekly therapy sessions for the family and/or the young person, but have no other specific therapy activities. They rely, rather, on the ongoing "intervention" of staff responding to successful behavior within the context of a competency-based milieu. Other residential programs, particularly those that operate within the "hospital" system, include therapy groups and other activities as part of the program.

Presumably, these differences in program structure reflect different ideas about what is necessary to bring about change as well as differences in history and development of the programs. Certainly, my own observations of different programs do not lead me to believe that "more is always better" as far as therapy activities are concerned. Many of the programs that include a larger number of types of therapy and groups seem to have evolved within a framework that was directed towards "acting on" clients, often from a more pathology-based perspective. If we see our role as that of "curing," it is tempting to believe that the more therapy activities we provide the greater the chance of success. Some of the apparently more effective programs I have witnessed seem quite "minimalist" in terms of structure. They reflect a belief that a group of staff that focuses on encouraging and highlighting difference and success within the (more or less) normal day-to-day activities can be just as successful in facilitating the process of people developing new views of themselves. That is, they trust the ideas, and the resources of their clients, rather than a set of strategies.

However, there is no right or wrong way to do residential treatment. Ultimately, whether or not there are group therapy sessions, or structured community meetings, or individual sessions, or whatever, is not the important issue. Different styles of programs operate equally helpfully in different places. What is important is that we consider the "climate" or the assumptions about whatever kinds of therapy activities we include in our program. If our aim is to create an environment that values clients' resources, that seeks to allow them to experience some control over the process of which they are part, and that seeks to assist the development of views of competence, then any activity should be considered in terms of how it furthers this aim. In summary, what is important is how we think about what we do.

INDIVIDUAL THERAPY

In many programs, the resident will meet regularly (often weekly) for an individual session. Hopefully, the content of these sessions will fit completely with the particular theme and the overall focus of the program rather than being experienced as a different kind of process. If the individual session appears to focus on "problem solving" or "addressing issues" it may easily undermine the practice and competency orientation of the rest of the program.

Hence, such individual sessions may have the same kinds of functions as those listed above for family sessions. Rather than seeing the sessions as "intervention," we might see them as times for reviewing goals and acknowledging progress. Staff will have been seeking to respond to exceptions and success throughout the day-to-day program, and the weekly sessions, being a little more structured, provide a good opportunity for reviewing these successes more explicitly, discussing their significance, and planning further practice to build upon them.

Natalie, age 16, was referred with a history of extremely aggressive behavior. She was described as "a hopeless case." During a couple of initial interviews, her interest in softball became apparent, and the theme for her placement that emerged from this was that of "batting for her life."

Natalie's time in the unit was one of practicing her batting skills and learning more about her own expertise in not "striking out." We acknowledged that, since this was a time of practice, the times when she struck out were learning times and not failures. As Natalie continued to respond to this theme, she and the staff continued to develop "softball language" together. Staff were able to respond to events by calling "strike 1 ... 2 ... 3" or "home run." Further, the goals that Natalie had identified as being what she would be doing when she was ready to leave were written on a large chart shaped like a softball diamond.

At weekly "key meetings" (therapy session with Natalie and her key worker), her progress was plotted around this diamond, enabling her to see her achievements towards her goals. These meetings did not have the tone of "working on serious issues." Rather, they took the form of reflecting back on the previous week, identifying the progress she had made and the times she had acted differently, how she had handled potential strike outs, when she had made runs, and so on.

Using our common language, I was able to ask her questions such as:

- How did you prepare yourself to hit the ball that far?
- It seems like you only just managed to hit that ball. What practice will you need to make a direct hit next time?
- How does it make a difference, knowing that you can hit a home run?
- Who will be the first person to notice your batting getting better? What will they notice?

As our discussions were built upon reviewing success and then discussing how these successes might make a difference in other situations, it was easier to warn against set-backs without seeming too pessimistic. After all, even the most skilled hitters miss the occasional ball, particularly fast or curve balls! Similarly, plotting her course around the diamond every week allowed Natalie to see her own overall progress, despite certain hiccups that might have happened during the week.

Natalie eventually moved into an apartment by herself and continued some contact with us as she told us of the ways that she was continuing to put into practice the skills she had learned.

—St. Stephen's Youth Accommodation Project,
Adelaide, South Australia

GROUP THERAPY FROM A COMPETENCY-BASED PERSPECTIVE

Group therapy sessions may be used usefully within a residential program. They have the benefit of harnessing the resources of the entire program community as well as helping peer interactions become more helpful.

Again, what is important is the focus of the groups. I have witnessed group sessions where the "agenda," explicit or otherwise, has been the latest problems that have arisen in the unit. The content of such groups has been either the latest problems encountered during visits home, the conflicts or failings that have become apparent within the program, nursing or residential staff members' observations about what issues the young person still needs "to work on," and so on.

Within a cooperative, competency-based approach, group sessions can become a powerful venue for highlighting success and discussing the significance of small steps towards goals.

The program includes two "process groups," morning and evening. When I first ran the "A.M. Process Group," I always began by asking the group "who needs to brag first about yesterday?" As the group members identified those who were successful, each member described what went well the previous day and was encouraged to set specific goals for this day. I often asked the person speaking to nominate who should talk next, based on what he or she had observed another resident doing better. I was amazed to see the atmosphere of these groups change as we focused on "what worked." At first, we found that the group leader needed to take a clear lead with talk of exceptions and bypass the tendency of patients to become problem-focused. Even comments like, "Gee, that sounds like it was terrible. So, how did you manage to get to this point by today?" can be important in helping change the focus. We have found that, over time, the groups have become more success-focused. Group members seem to enjoy finding good things to say about one another!

Sometimes, a group member has been encouraged to ask other residents to help, by "pointing out when I don't seem so depressed," "letting me know when you think I'm not being so irritating," and so on. This process encourages much more positive peer interactions. We also use a "scale" for members to scale where they see themselves (in terms of a particular goal) and set an immediate goal in terms of where they would like to be at the end of the day and, again, others may contribute to "noticing" steps in the right direction (see Figure 11.1).

The "P.M. Process Group," at the end of the day, involves members talking about where they saw themselves move to during the day. This has been fairly structured although, in an adolescent unit, this has evolved more into a "community group," where the adolescents discuss each other and their days. Of course, they have shown the typical adolescent tendency to confront and/or become defensive. However, gentle persistence by the leaders asking questions about exceptions has gradually eliminated the conflict in these groups and allowed them to provide crucial validation to one another of their struggles and experiences.

The children's unit has more explicitly used the technique of "exter-

MORNING/EVENING PROCESS GROUPS

Daily goal-setting is a way of achieving, in a short time, what's really important. These groups will meet daily.

A.M. Process Group

Date: _____

Goal for today: _____

1. How have you minimally or successfully accomplished this goal in the past?

2. How were you wise enough to accomplish it in this way?

3. Of these strategies you have used before, which one will you use today?

4. On a scale of 1-10 ("1" being completely impossible and "10" being completely successful), where would you like to be at the end of today?

P.M. Process Group

5. On the scale in Question 4, how close did you get to your goal? How did you manage that?

6. Ask your group members what changes they noticed in you today as you moved towards your goal.

© 1992, Linda Metcalf. Slightly adapted and used with permission.

FIGURE 11.1:   A Form Used in Morning and Evening "Process Groups" in a Residential Program

nalizing the problem." We have had the children draw the problem ("the anger," "the fears," or whatever) but draw it as it will look when they have defeated it. These drawings are glued onto a magnet and the magnet can be moved along the scale, which might look like a rainbow, a train track, etc., on a magnetic board.

—Linda Metcalf, Arlington, Texas

In this particular unit, "process groups" had been a part of the program for some time, and there was never any question that they would not continue. The staff involved, however, sought to "reframe" these groups so that they would fit within the more competency-based or solution-focused orientation that the program was adopting. The description above demonstrates that it was not a matter of changing the entire structure of the groups, rather it entailed thinking about their emphasis and the kinds of issues they addressed.

Figure 11.2 shows the form developed within the same program for use in "anger groups." Again, these groups were preexisting, and the program designer sought to "refocus" them so that they provided opportunities for members to focus on success and practical strategies rather than on notions of "working through" anger. In these particular groups, "anger" was externalized, and the content of the groups focused on residents' successes in not allowing anger to take over.

THERAPY IS NOTHING SPECIAL

It is easy for us therapists to become overly concerned with the importance of what we do behind the closed doors of the therapy room. This cooperative, competency-based approach to residential treatment seeks to show that the entire program is part of the "therapy" process and that the seemingly mundane interactions residential staff have with residents and with parents are just as important as more formal therapy activities. Of course, this requires that we therapists be prepared to "let go" a little of our sense of our own importance. Some of the most apparently successful programs I have seen have been programs where the therapists have seen their role primarily as one of supporting the residential staff. Some of the least successful were programs where therapists have clung to the notion that their job is *the* crucial one, as if something "magical" happens in therapy rooms.

Therapy *is* an important component of the residential process, yet it is only one part of that process. Particularly with children and adolescents, I am sure that the most meaningful interactions are those that happen around the normal life experiences (mealtimes, playing games, doing household chores, and so on). In this context, "therapy" is primarily an opportunity to exchange information, highlight success, and establish further goals.

ANGER GROUP

"Anger" plagues everyone once in a while. A method of venting and airing feelings, it can be a healthy release. Sometimes, however, "anger" creates problems in our lives, which distance us from others, threaten physical harm or sabotage our future plans and relationships. The "anger group" aims to help you look at times when you did not let "anger" interfere with your life. No one can be angry 100% of the time. Our aim in this group is to identify times when you were angry, but used good strategies to make sure the "anger" did not take over.

Use the chart below to help identify "triggers" anger uses and how you have prevented "anger" from attacking your life.

SITUATIONS WHICH ENCOURAGE ANGER TO TAKE OVER (When anger tried to control me)	SITUATIONS WHERE ANGER WAS NOT SUCCESSFUL (How I controlled anger)
1. _____	1. _____
2. _____	2. _____
3. _____	3. _____
4. _____	4. _____
5. _____	5. _____

A. In what situation today would you like to be more in control of your anger?

   _____

B. When was the last time you were successful at controlling it?

   _____

C. How did you do this?

   _____

D. What is your plan for today, based on how you controlled "anger" in the past?

   _____

E. On a scale of 1 to 10 (1 is "anger is completely in control" and 10 is "I am completely in control"), where are you now? _____
As you try the things that have worked before, where would you like to be by _____ (tonight, this weekend, etc.)? _____

FIGURE 11.2:   A Form Used in "Anger Groups"

12

COMPLETION and
CELEBRATION: EMBARKING
on the NEW FUTURE

Transition and practice is a finite process. Making and consolidating changes and dealing with problem situations will go on forever and, in some ways, the challenges that have been part of the process of therapy will continue even after therapy finishes. However, our aim is that, at the end of the residential placement, families will have been helped to experience themselves as competent and resourceful and so be able to continue to meet these challenges themselves. That is, the focused, change-oriented tasks of residential treatment will give way to the ongoing tasks and "ups and downs" that will continue in day-to-day life.

Framing the residential placement as a period of transition allows us to consider the process finishing *not* when all is resolved but when family members are ready to embark upon the next stage. If treatment is success-ful, this "success" will be shown not in every difficulty being solved, but in the success of developing a new view of self and the future.

As the various aspects of the residential program have proceeded, their focus has been on practicing and equipping. If goals have been set using considerations such as, "How will you know when you are ready to keep on with this at home?" or if the theme has provided a sense of training or preparing, then it will become time to "move on." The future focus of the program will mean that staff will have responded at times to various events and achievements by asking how they will make a difference once the young person returns home. Thus, returning home will be the natural, next step. Parents and young person will probably (and understandably) feel a degree of trepidation about this step, and it is important that their uncertainty be validated. Nonetheless, a program that has preserved a focus on the new future is likely to find all parties more agreeable to discharge (as opposed to a program that has focused only on bringing about changes during the admission itself, which is likely to find that parents need "convincing" that the problem is solved).

Preparing for Discharge

In a sense, if the residential program is seen as a time of transition, then every aspect of it, from the moment of admission, has been preparing for discharge. Nonetheless, staff and clients will begin to consider discharge more explicitly as time passes.

As the program proceeds, staff can encourage the resident to think about such questions as:

- How do you think your success today will make it easier for you to go back home?
- You've really shown that you can get on differently with the other kids here. What are some of the ways you will be able to use these ideas back at school?
- It's great that things went better when you went home for the weekend. What did you do differently? What did your parents do differently? So, what do you think it will be like when you and they are able to get on like that full-time?
- Let's imagine that you are able to do what you did here today when you get back home. How do you think it will make things different for you and your parents?

Similar questions may be asked in therapy sessions involving the parents.

As progress is reviewed during the placement, goals can be "updated" with questions such as, "We've seen how you've been practicing controlling your anger. How do you think you'll know when you're ready to get on with doing that at home?" or "It's great that you are able to appreciate John's steps forward in controlling his anger. How do you think you'll know that he's ready to keep doing that at home?"

The aim is continually to invite them to think about the present changes and achievements in terms of their future together.

Completion of Practice

The theme and the goals will determine when the stage of completion has been reached. It is preferable not to have a predetermined time period for the placement but to allow progress toward the goals to determine the time for discharge.

Describing the "reincorporation phase" of the ritual process, Roberts (1988) says:

> In the third ritual phase . . . people are connected back to the community in their new status. In therapy, there is a move away from the special place and time of therapy towards connections to family resources and their day-to-day life. (p. 40)

As this time arrives, the task becomes one of reviewing and highlighting changes and beginning to place them within the context of ongoing, everyday life. The residential program has been an "abnormal" environment, with a more limited focus than will be the case back at home. The therapeutic task becomes one of connecting what has occurred during this transition to the realities of the future, and to do so in a way that highlights a change in status.

Certain specific parts of the program will end, such as particular tasks, charts, or experiments, and the declaring of these as over provides a useful way of reviewing and highlighting. In a final therapy session (or sessions) before discharge, the young person and family members may be asked to review the placement and identify differences between their state at the time of admission and their state now. They may be asked to speculate on the ways that these changes will make a difference in various aspects of their ongoing lives together—school, family, and so on.

I often find it helpful to ask questions such as, "Suppose someone who hasn't seen you for a while and who does not even know you have been in this residential unit visits your family. What do you suppose they will notice that is different? What do you think that will tell them about you?"

REPORTING ON CHANGES

When reports need to be written (be they for courts or welfare departments, referring agencies, or professionals who will be involved in follow-up), I find it most useful to involve the clients in writing such reports. This has the effect of providing an opportunity to review progress, of confirming the clients' own expertise as the best judges of their own success, and (hopefully) inviting the recipients of the reports to begin to view the clients in a new light.

In such a session, the young person and parents may be asked to describe all the ways that they think things are now different. Since this report is for an external agency, they are encouraged to be as specific and as detailed as possible. As change proceeds, it is easy for people to "take it for granted" and so be less aware of the significance of the changes they have achieved. The requirements of writing a report "force" all participants to be more explicit about the changes. In doing so, they may "discover" changes that had been forgotten or had been disregarded, and these changes help consolidate their emerging views of themselves as competent.

They may then be asked to describe those things that demonstrate their readiness for discharge and similarly to elaborate them for the sake of the readers of the report. The discussion may proceed with the clients setting their own follow-up plans, as they are asked to consider the challenges that lie ahead and the ways that the things they have achieved will equip them for these.

In my own therapy practice, I usually involve my clients in writing reports in this manner. The process appears to be a helpful way of affirming their new status as experts. I may then rewrite the report to ensure that it is the "correct" format, although I always make it clear that it has been written cooperatively. I use such phrases as :

- These are the changes that the family and I believe have been achieved . . .
- Bill believes that he is unlikely to commit such an offense again. He believes that the following changes that he has achieved during his treatment support this confidence. . . . His parents and I have seen evidence of these changes.
- The family have identified the following issues with which they feel they may need ongoing support as they continue to implement these changes in their home situation. . . . This agency has agreed to offer follow-up counseling to assist them in monitoring their ongoing success.

As a matter of practice, I give a copy of any such report to the family. In fact, I often invite the family to mail the report to the appropriate person, perhaps with a covering letter of their own.

HELPING OTHER PEOPLE NOTICE

As the young person leaves the program, he or she will resume contact with a variety of other agencies and institutions that will have some influence on his or her future. We have seen that an important part of the therapy process for adolescent and family is that of helping them *notice* those small examples of success or change. Similarly, the main aspect of the influence of such institutions as schools, probation officers, welfare department officers, and so on, is whether or not they are able to notice and respond to emerging changes.

It is understandable that, for example, a young person's school may have developed a view of him or her as "difficult" or "disturbed." While they may be pleased that the adolescent is receiving treatment, this fact in itself may strengthen their view of the problem. Unless this view is changed, it is inevitable that they will be on the lookout for any small signs that the problem has not been solved. Even worse, some schools accept the young person back explicitly for a "trial period," and this is usually setting them up to look for failure.

In discharging a resident, it is important to consider how best to help outside agencies notice the changes that have occurred. One way is to invite such people to attend discharge celebrations or to provide reports similar to those described above. We need to think of other ways to invite such people to notice and respond to success rather than failure.

Schools in Australia often use "behavior charts" to monitor the behavior of troublesome students. These are cards on which the teacher is invited to write a comment about the student at the end of each lesson. The card is taken to the School Principal at the end of each day and then taken home to be read and signed by parents. The problem with these cards is that they are only used for students who are identified as problems, and teachers all know this. Thus, the very appearance of such a card is often a "signal" that this is a troublesome student and so often an invitation to find something to criticize.

As I approached the end of therapy with one young man, Justin, I was concerned that his return to school might be greeted by a search for evidence of failure. I spoke to the school, explaining that part of the emphasis in therapy had been on Justin monitoring his own behavior and taking responsibility for himself. (We had not used this specific language during therapy; however, it was important in this conversation that I express my request in language that would be meaningful to the school personnel). I asked if the school would be willing to provide opportunities for him to continue these skills. When the school principal agreed that they would be happy to do so, I asked if they would give Justin a set of "behavior chart" cards on which he was to write comments, at the end of each lesson, about his own behavior. The principal agreed, although I could sense over the phone his skepticism about whether Justin would complete this task or how seriously he would take it. I suggested that Justin might show the principal his card at the end of each day and take it home to show his parents.

I had discussed this plan with Justin, who was also concerned that the teachers would be "out to get him." He carried out the task, although his comments about his own behavior during the first few days were hardly profound. Nonetheless, when he showed the principal his card, on which he had written comments such as "very well behaved," "showed great improvement," and so on, the principal was delighted. After a week or so, when Justin began writing more critical comments about his behavior ("Talked too much in class," "Did not apply himself this class"), the principal was even happier. Of course, these comments were exactly the kind that, had they been written by a teacher, would have led to Justin being lectured and perhaps threatened with suspension from school. However, framed in this manner, this exercise encouraged the principal to respond positively to Justin's efforts.

Whereas Justin had returned to school for a three month "trial period," the principal was so happy with Justin's "self-monitoring" that he ended the trial period after only a few weeks.

It seems to be human nature that, once we know someone has (or has had) a problem, we are more likely to see evidence of it and less likely to notice anything that is different. Every school student is familiar with the effect of a student gaining a "reputation" within the school. Thirty students may be misbehaving, but it is the one who is "known" as a troublemaker who will be noticed. Therefore, an important way to help residents with their reintroduction to school and other situations is to find ways to encourage such people to notice evidence of change.

Celebrating Success

Once the young person and family have begun to think more about their new future and we have made plans with them for how they will continue to move forward together, discharge is worth celebrating. A characteristic I have noticed of residential staff the world over is that they seem to enjoy parties! Discharge is an obvious excuse for a party — however, the discharge celebration has a serious purpose.

The rite of passage is the whole process of transition from one status to a new status, and we have considered every aspect of the program as part of this "ritual" process. The completion of the process is often marked by a celebration. This may be a ritual in itself, in that it is a purposeful symbolization of what has been achieved, but it is also the public declaration of the entire transition process. As mentioned previously, graduation ceremonies, weddings, and initiation ceremonies are ritual celebrations and proclamations of the transition from one status to another.

A discharge celebration is a way of declaring the new status of family and young person, of making it public so that they may be seen in a new light. It also marks the change for them and helps them consolidate their own new view of themselves.

The celebration does not need to be complex, but it is more than just party food and decorations. The proceedings might include short speeches, in which changes and success are highlighted. In units where themes have been commonplace, other residents may be asked to say something about the success of the young person who is leaving. Presentations may include certificates or symbolic gifts or trophies.

Tracy, age 15, had been sexually abused but not believed after reporting it; she came to us unforgiving and angry, verbally and aggressively loud. She saw no benefit in telling the truth, so building an honest trusting relationship with staff took a long time.

Various approaches to dealing with her desire to run from her problems, her anger, and so on, were tried, but with only limited success. In previous therapy, she had been given licence to express her feelings in the group, but had no idea what to do with these feelings once expressed and was unable to control her expression of anger. Both staff and residents received verbal abuse and were ordered around; there were slamming doors and constant yelling in the house.

Tracy made some progress in terms of talking through her problems and dealing with strong feelings by such activities as going for walks. Unfortunately, her behavior led to difficulties with other residents, and her previous pattern of running away returned. Tracy chose to leave the program rather than allow relationships to deteriorate further.

Even in such a situation, it was appropriate to "mark" her leaving and seek to place it within a positive frame. We were able to highlight the various successes she had achieved and commented that these made us hopeful that Tracy would not continue with her lifestyle of running away. Her leaving was framed as being a considered decision rather than a "spur of the moment running away," and helped us be confident that she could begin facing up to her problems and settle down somewhere.

We gave Tracy a magnet with a sneaker on it, so that wherever she went she could display it prominently to remind her that we had seen her on many occasions facing up to conflict and problems—she could do it! Our aim was to give her something that symbolized this leaving as different to previous ones. It signified the beginning of a different future.

Some time later, Tracy phoned us from another state to tell us she had found a relative and decided to settle down, and face up to things in her life and was receiving counseling. She was excited to tell us that she was not wearing out the soles of her sneakers from running away any more!

— *"The Anchor," Presbyterian Social Service Department, Sydney*

Discharge celebrations will usually be just that — celebrations that mark success. However, if we think of them as ritual markers of change, they can be just as important in situations that have not ended as we might have hoped. The "celebration" in this example enabled staff and resident to place her leaving within a more optimistic frame. She didn't leave feeling she was a failure, but with this decision framed as a new step. The gift of the sneaker-magnet was an ongoing symbol of this, and her later comment suggested that it remained a meaningful symbol to her.

Some examples of other symbolic gifts or trophies are:

- a key (the "key to the future"), signifying a young person's successful practice in learning to choose her own directions ("her own doors to open")
- a poster of a surfboard rider — "Kevin has shown that he has learned to stand up as he rides the waves" (this young man, interested in surfing, had learned to "stand on his own two feet")
- various certificates that develop naturally from themes — "Champion Grower Upper," "Expert Fear Fighter," and so on
- sporting trophies, suitably engraved
- a beach towel, for someone who has learned to swim rather than sink

A CELEBRATION

Towards the end of Chapter 2 is part of the story of David, a 12-year-old boy whose residential placement was framed as practice in "taming his temper" and whose interest in boxing led youth workers to use such expressions as "the temper having him on the ropes" or "having the temper down for the count."

When David was discharged, his family joined the staff and residents for a celebration to mark the changes that had been achieved. The residential unit was decorated by David and the other residents, and those present assembled for the "formalities."

Youth worker: I'd like to welcome everyone to David's party, which is being held to celebrate David and his family being successful in the first round in the battle against his temper. David came to Timaru to get practice in taming his temper and growing up to be 12 on the inside. It hasn't always been easy, with a heavy-weight opponent, but he has persevered with his training and showed us all that he is prepared to make a good effort. (*applause*)

The temper has sometimes almost had David down on the canvas but he has learned how to get up and overpower it. It still has some strength left, but David is determined to keep going until he finally has it out for the count. With his own hard work, and the hard work and support of his family, we are confident he will go on to win the championship.

Bill (another resident): Me and David have been friends and roommates, and I've seen how hard he's worked on his temper. Here you are, David. (*gives David the trophy*)

David: Thanks, Bill. I just hope that my temper doesn't come out any more and that I keep controlling it.

(*applause*)

Therapist: When David came in, it was clear that the temper was making it difficult for the family to live together at home. Then everyone in the family made a big decision that they wanted things to go differently. It's been a family effort. You've heard from Helen a bit about what David's done while he's been here and how he's figured out ways to beat his temper and grow up on the inside. He's kept monitoring his temper danger on his chart every day, and he's been doing that himself to help him know how strong he's getting. I'd also like to congratulate Mary and Robert for the work they've done in coaching David in his growing up and temper taming. They've been trying things like ignoring the temper and not letting it get on top of them, not giving in to it but being firm, and practicing working together to show David how united they are. I'd like to congratulate you all for what you've done and for being so sure that you're ready to keep on at home.

I'd like to present David with this certificate, which says, "This is to certify that David has completed his training in temper taming and growing up, and is hereby qualified to continue practice full-time at home."

I'd also like to present this certificate to Mary and Robert, "This is to certify that Mary and Robert have become fully qualified temper taming and growing up coaches."

(*applause*)

Mother: I'd just like to say thank you to everyone for their help to all of us and for helping us see that we can do it together.

Another youth worker explained about the two empty plaques on the trophy—one plaque had been engraved to show David's success, but the other two were for the two "rounds" yet to be fought and the family would decide (perhaps in the course of follow-up counseling sessions) when these warranted engraving.

On the table was David's cake, decorated to depict the "Temper Danger Level" chart he had been using. David was invited ceremonially to cut the cake, signifying that he no longer needs the assistance of the chart but can continue to monitor his behavior himself.

The party then proceeded, with David and his family, staff, and other residents enjoying cake and other treats, and finished with group photographs of David and his family with their trophy and certificates.

After Discharge

After discharge, the process will most likely entail some kind of follow-up therapy. The period of transition is over, and therapy should proceed on the basis of the expectation that changes will be consolidated. (If therapists *expect* continued success and use language that reflects this expectation—without, of course, applying pressure—clients are more likely to report success!). That is, the task is no longer one of *finding* solutions but one of continuing to implement those solutions that have been developed.

Of course, there will be new issues and difficulties that will arise; nonetheless, the task of the therapist is to treat the family according to its new status. Family members have been through a transition and have attained a new status. This is now "the real world" (in a way that the residential program could never be) but the new challenges that arise do not alter the achievements that they have made. Parents and young person may be asked to suggest their own solutions to newly arising difficulties, on the basis of the things they have practiced. A therapist will continue to observe and suggest, but he or she should ensure that this is done in a way that confirms the new status of competence.

In many ways, the task of follow-up therapy is simply to help family members notice ongoing success. Following de Shazer (1991), the therapist might ask, "So, what has been going better since you left here?" rather than "How have things been?" The latter question invites a comparison between things that have gone better and things that have gone worse. The first question, on the other hand, presupposes improvement and leaves the clients having to select which of the things that have "gone better" they will mention. The more we make it likely that they will relate improvement, the more likely it is that they will be able to notice ongoing change. The more they notice ongoing change, the more they will respond to it (and reinforce it) in their daily interactions. At the same time, of course, it is important not to appear to be dismissing parents' continued concerns.

COMPLETING TRANSITION . . . BUT NOT RETURNING HOME

Some programs are longer term and may not necessarily involve the young person returning home to his or her parents. I know a number of programs that have a substantial "accommodation" function and include the expectation of the resident remaining for one or two years. Often, these involve living-skills programs, work-preparation, and other activities that are practical steps towards an ongoing successful life. Others are "pre-foster care" programs, where the length of stay is often prolonged by the unavailability of a suitable foster placement.

If a young person is likely to remain in the residential unit for a prolonged period, it is not helpful for the therapeutic program to continue indefinitely. The notion of "transition" entails a defined period of practice or experimenting, which provides a basis from which the person may pursue his or her life more successfully. The period of transition should not be prolonged, otherwise the person does not have the opportunity to experience him or herself as having achieved a new status. If the "transition" continues throughout a longer placement, the young person is likely to feel frustrated and changes are likely to begin to disappear.

So, how do we deal with those situations where external circumstances prevent discharge?

It is most helpful that we still frame the placement, initially, as a period of "practice or experimenting," with clear goals and an overt "therapeutic" focus. However, this need not last for the whole period in the unit. It is still important that transition finish, and its completion be marked ritually. Afterwards, the young person may remain in the residential unit but the emphasis is different.

I know a number of programs that have dealt with this issue in a number of ways:

- After the period of transition, the next phase involves the ongoing living-skills and work-preparation programs.
- One program had residents initially sleeping on the first floor. Following the completion of transition, they moved to the second floor and had their own room.

- In some programs, the post-transition phase entails a lesser degree of supervision. The young people are treated much more like "residents" than "patients."

It is important that, once change has been recognized and the process of "moving on" has been acknowledged, that the language of the experimental phase be dispensed with. The young person will still face challenges and struggles, and there may be ongoing issues that warrant therapy, however the language of "practice," "experiment," and so on, and the language associated with the particular theme or frame, should give way to more everyday language.

How Long Is Long Enough?

What constitutes "long enough"? That is a good question, since residential placements vary in length and different programs operate under different constraints. My observation has been that programs that have adopted the kinds of ideas described in this book have seen their average length-of-stay reduced considerably. It is not uncommon to find adolescent programs where the period of "transition" (and, so, of placement) lasts six to eight weeks. One program, represented in a few of the examples earlier in this book, deals with often long-term adult drug and alcohol users and has a length of stay of around three weeks.

If a program is designed to "cure" problems, it can seem to go on forever, and there is often a debate about whether or not the end has been reached. If a program has a predetermined length, problems seem often to "expand" to fill the available time. The length of placement should be determined by the goals, and it is probably more helpful for staff to assume these goals will be reached sooner rather than later.

13

CONCLUSION

As mentioned in Chapter 1, residential treatment need not be a "second best" form of treatment. When it is necessary for a family member to have a period away from home in a program that reflects a cooperative, competency-based approach, residential treatment can help children or adolescents and their parents develop a new view of themselves.

On the other hand, when residential treatment is concerned with control and cure, when it seeks to solve problems or repair deficits, it can be a powerful factor in further disempowering families and contributing to problems persisting or recurring.

Whether we acknowledge it or not, any therapeutic work we do with families or family members will reflect our basic assumptions and our ways of thinking about what we do. There is no such thing as a "neutral" program or activity. Nothing we do can be dismissed as simply "looking after" the young people, dealing with "practical (and not therapeutic) concerns," or "just meeting physical needs," without being considered in terms of the overall context of our involvement. Every aspect of the program, no matter how small or seemingly insignificant, will either contribute to new views of competence and optimism or will exacerbate old views of failure and incompetence.

Pervasive Pessimism

I have encountered staff from a number of residential programs who seem afflicted with pessimism about the futures of the young people in their care. It is true that many of the children, adolescents, and adults who come into a residential program bring with them histories of violence or abuse, numerous experiences of neglect, rejection, and failure, and often longstanding substance abuse, many encounters with the law or a myriad of unsuccessful treatment experiences. Whether they present as angry or as subdued, they are often overwhelmed by the difficulties of themselves *and the system*. Their parents, if they are involved, are similarly overwhelmed and disheartened. It is easy for those of us who work with these people to become equally overwhelmed and disheartened.

My concern about some approaches to residential treatment is that they institutionalize pessimism. It is not that residential treatment itself is second best—rather, the expectations some programs seem to have about outcome seem second best. If we expect that we, and our clients, will fail then that is most likely what will happen. "Without the expectation that things can get better, therapy makes no sense" (de Shazer, 1988, p. 191).

What Have Atoms to Do With Residential Treatment?

A competency-based perspective is not simply a matter of looking at our work through "rose-colored glasses." Rather, this perspective focuses on competence and strength and believes that they exist in our clients, no matter how "difficult," "disturbed," or "uncooperative" they may appear.

My own professional discipline (psychology) has spent the last few decades trying to establish its scientific respectability. That is, it seems to have sought to become more and more precise in its explanation of human behavior. If we can explain particular behaviors precisely, then we believe we can classify them and that the classification will help us know how to deal with them. This is what diagnosis is all about. In medicine, it is important to know exactly what the diagnosis is—what type of bacteria are involved, which organ is malfunctioning, and so on—for the diagnosis tells us the appropriate treatment. Classification and diagnosis in psychiatry and psychology (and practiced in some residential programs) aspires to the same level of accurate detection on the assumption that once we "know" exactly what the problem is (and what it is not), we can "know" the correct treatment.

I find it intriguing that, at exactly the same time as the psychology and mental health disciplines are pursuing greater and greater certainty and exactness, many people within the so-called "hard sciences" are acknowledging that such precision is impossible. Physics has been engaged in a similar search for precise explanation, as demonstrated in its search for the "fundamental particles"—the ultimate building blocks of matter and life. When physicists discovered atoms, they thought they had found the fundamental particles and so could explain everything in terms of the properties of atoms. Unfortunately, their certainty was short-lived since physicists went on to discover that atoms were made up of protons, neutrons, and electrons. If *these* were the fundamental particles, then we could explain everything in the universe in terms of their properties. The search for precise explanation did not stop there, however, and later physicists discovered that protons, neutrons, and electrons are themselves made up of even smaller particles. The search continued since, once we find the fundamental particles, then we can be exact in our explanation of everything in the universe.

As this search continued, physics began to come unstuck! Quantum physicists discovered that they *could* find even smaller, more elementary particles. Unfortunately, they also discovered that they *could not* measure or describe these particles completely. In order to describe a particle completely, a scientist has to be able to measure its momentum and its position. Once these are measured, then everything else about the particle is apparent. What they discovered was that it is impossible to measure both the momentum and the position of a subatomic (quantum) particle. In fact, Heisenberg showed that if we establish the momentum of a particle, we *cannot* know its position (since measuring its momentum actually changes its position). Or, if we establish the position of a particle, we *cannot* know its momentum (since measuring its position actually changes its momentum).

This finding has been encapsulated in Heisenberg's Uncertainty Principle, which has changed many of the assumptions underlying modern physics (Heisenberg, 1958). Paraphrased, it says that the closer we get to *the* exact explanation, the more uncertain we must be about it. Further, this idea says that our processes of measuring or identifying these particles actually change them. That is, our observations or measurements are not neutral but affect the things we are observing.

Some quantum physicists have gone even further. They have suggested that these subatomic particles *only actually exist* when we measure or observe them. Beyond that, we cannot know where, or whether, they are. This theory is perhaps somewhat esoteric, however it is a reminder that our process of observing actually affects the thing we are observing.

We do not admit subatomic particles into our residential programs; nonetheless, the conclusions of quantum physics provide an interesting parallel to our quest for certainty. Physicists have a choice. They can either choose to see a particle in terms of its momentum *or* they can choose to see it in terms of its position (and each, without the other, has quite different implications).

In fact, physics says even more about our choice in how we see things. Elementary particles moving through space-time may be viewed as particles or as waves. Light, for example, may be viewed as light-waves or it may be viewed as particles (photons). Both are equally "true" (that is, both accord with what physicists can observe) but both have very different implications in particular circumstances, and scientists have a choice as to which way they wish to view things at any particular time—and the "things" will tend to behave according to the way the scientists choose to observe them.

> How can mutually exclusive wave-like and particle-like behaviors both be properties of one and the same light? They are not properties of light. They are properties of our interaction with light. Depending upon our choice of experiment, we can cause light to manifest either particle-like properties or wave-like properties. (Zukav, 1979, p. 116)

If this degree of uncertainty, and of choice in how we see things, is true at the subatomic level then we might expect it to be even more true when we are dealing with more complex beings (such as adolescents and families). For "momentum" and "position," or for "wave" and "particle," we might equally substitute "pathology" and "competence."

Hence, nothing is certain—we have a choice about how we wish to view the people with whom we work. We can either view them as manifestations of pathology and deficit *or* we can view them as representing a degree of competence and skill. We cannot do both. Further, *if we choose* to view them in terms of pathology, then the focus on problems that this perspective requires makes it much more difficult for us to recognize their strengths and resources. On the other hand, *if we choose* to view them as competent and resourceful, then our focus on strengths is more likely to obscure their deficits from our view.

That is, in thinking about the young people and their families who present at our residential facilities, the way we (choose to) view them will have an impact on the way they are. My experience is that, the more I strive (and, sometimes, struggle) to see my clients as competent and successful so the more they tend to demonstrate these characteristics (and, at the same time, the more I simply don't notice their deficits or pathology).

MEANING VS. EMOTION

The chapters of this book have said much about peoples' "experience" yet little overtly about peoples' "feelings." Does this approach ignore feelings? Of course not. It would be unrealistic to ignore the fact that children, adolescents, and their families who have had longstanding difficulties *feel* a wide range of emotions. The experiences they have had of struggling with difficulties, perhaps having unsuccessful encounters with other therapists and professionals, and of coming to the point of considering a residential admission will have been accompanied by feelings of failure, incompetence, guilt, frustration, and despair. The antecedents of the situation, perhaps involving physical or sexual abuse, separation of parents or spouse, economic and social pressures, and so on, will have promoted further feelings that may have been major contributors to the way people currently view themselves and the situation. Whatever a "theory" might say, common sense says that we cannot ignore such feelings.

I have suggested earlier that the process of constructing a theme for a placement must be built upon family members experiencing themselves as being heard and their feelings being validated. They need to know that we are genuinely concerned about them and their predicament. Nothing in the range of the brief or family therapies changes what we already know about people needing to feel validated, to experience empathic responses from the professionals with whom they have contact. Anything less becomes the application of technique without any real respect or genuineness.

The question becomes one not of "*Do* we take feelings into account?" but rather "*How* do we take them into account?" My belief is that acknowledgment of feelings is crucial but is not in itself what brings about change. Feelings are one manifestation of a person's constructs or view of self. That is, how I *feel* in a particular situation will depend upon how I make sense of myself and the situation. Thus, a change of feelings requires a change in constructs in the same way as does a change in behavior.

The expression of feelings may not in itself be helpful, although it may be a helpful part of the process. Certainly, I believe that any helpful aspects of the expression of feelings are often negated by the prescription to our clients that they *must* do this. I have said earlier that any process in which we prescribe what our clients must do carries the risk of confirming their lack of expertise and competence.

In considering therapy with young people who have experienced sexual abuse, I have suggested elsewhere that

> There is widespread agreement that young people who have been victims of abuse can benefit from opportunities to talk about their experiences but it may be unhelpful for this to be the primary and initial focus of therapy. If young people are experiencing themselves within a context of "out-of-controlness," encouragement to "get it all out" may lead to their being faced with a wealth of emotion inside themselves that equally

feels out of their control. Such out-of-control feelings are terrifying and perpetuate the general context of their experience. Thus, getting feelings out at this stage may confirm their ideas that their feelings are beyond their control and further entrench their distress. (Durrant, 1987, p. 60)

This is an important consideration both for how we conduct therapy or therapy groups within the residential context and for the expectations we have of the behavior of residents who have had emotionally traumatic experiences.

For example, let us consider a residential unit that includes a number of young people who have backgrounds of violence and abuse. I have suggested that, often, their view of themselves is one that includes the idea that they are unable to experience any control over their angry and painful emotions and impulses. If the residential program operates on the assumption that these residents benefit from expressing their anger, and that this is the way to help them work through it, then we might expect the residents to display a high degree of violent behavior. I have seen programs that tolerate such behavior, since they see this sort of expression as therapeutic. My concern is that the simple expression of these feelings through such behavior exacerbates the idea that the clients have no control over these emotions. Such continued experiences of "out-of-control-ness" are hardly conducive to feeling better or developing greater confidence or self-esteem. Further, the violence inevitably seems to escalate until it reaches a point where staff are forced to step in and take control. The consequences of this step can be disastrous, since it easily leaves young people feeling, "I am dangerous. I need other people to step in and take control."

Expression of emotion, like everything else I have discussed, needs to be considered in terms of the context or meaning-frame within which it occurs and which it, in turn, may perpetuate. My approach to therapy and to residential treatment does not see emotion as paramount, nor does it see behavior as paramount. We must acknowledge emotion in order that people feel heard and respected. We focus on changes in behavior since they are tangible and observable. Both are aspects of our aim to help develop new views of self.

Thinking Differently

This book has sought to present ideas about residential treatment from a perspective that harnesses clients' competence and successes. Such a perspective naturally leads to a more cooperative relationship with our clients, since they are able to experience themselves as part of the process rather than subjects of it.

I have suggested that this perspective is most easily facilitated by an approach to residential programming that sees the residential placement as a period of transition, an experimental phase during which residents and families develop and "practice" their new status. The idea of the placement as transition rather than as cure relieves the pressure from residential staff to solve the complex problems with which they are presented. This does not mean a "hands off" role, but envisages a role in which staff are not the agents of change but the active contributors to a context that promotes change. Their role is one of noticing, highlighting, and responding to behavior in ways that allow clients to experience greater confidence, self-control, and choice.

The various situations, ideas and examples have demonstrated different ways that this perspective might make a difference to daily programs, discipline, and consequences, interaction with parents and other family members, specific therapy activities, and staff and program management.

What is common to the various aspects presented throughout the book is that the staff involved have sought to *think* differently about what they do. Some examples appear dramatic, others are apparently more mundane. Ultimately, what this book is about is the way we think rather than what we do.

THINKING DIFFERENTLY — AN EXERCISE

The suggestion that we should be thinking differently applies to the whole process of residential treatment. However, it is also applicable in those particular situations where staff find themselves "stuck" with a particular resident. As I have suggested, residential staff, like parents, often find themselves stuck in "more of the same" patterns. That is, when faced with a particularly difficult young person, a seeming impasse, or a situation that continues to escalate, they easily keep thinking, and reacting, in the same way that does not seem to be working. In such situations, thinking differently is not always easy.

I have used a group exercise in training residential staff that seeks to address this issue. Some staff groups have reported that they have used this exercise in staff meetings or case reviews when they have found themselves stuck.

Describe the situation or resident with which you are experiencing particular difficulty. Try to describe the situation as specifically as possible, in terms of what happens and what you and the child/adolescent actually do. Then consider the following questions:

1. How do you *typically* make sense of this situation—how do you usually describe the behavior, what motivation do you usually attribute to the young person, etc.? For example, how do you talk about the young person or situation when you are "complaining" to your coworkers about it?
2. How does the way that you make sense of, and describe, the situation contribute to your keeping on trying the same responses—how does it help you keep stuck?
3. How could you make sense of the situation differently—for example, could you describe the behavior or motivation more positively? (For the moment, try to ignore whether or not you "believe" these alternate explanations. Just try to come up with as many as possible.)
4. If you were to decide to act according to one of these alternate explanations, how might it make a difference in how you approach the situation? (Again, try to put aside your natural reactions of, "But what about . . . ?" or "It would never work because . . . ")

What is important about this procedure is finding ways to think differently and consider how they might lead to different action. After this discussion, it can be useful to reflect on the process of the discussion by asking,

5. "What question or questions was it most helpful to ask ourselves in order to be able to think differently about the situation?"

An exercise such as this can be helpful in "brainstorming" a variety of possible approaches. It may be that none of the specific ideas will be able to be used; however, the process of thinking differently is useful in itself, and staff are more likely to come up with other ideas later.

You Don't Have to Be Stunningly Creative . . . Just Patiently Persistent

As I have had the opportunity to share ideas with staff from a variety of residential programs who have been experimenting with competency-based perspectives, some of which are represented in this book, I have often felt daunted by their creativity. I have witnessed creative examples of discipline, "catchy" themes for placements, and innovative program activities. In sharing some of these examples with you, the reader, my fear has been that you will feel that your program must show the same degree of "cleverness." When I aspire to cleverness, I usually fail and, often, revert back to what I always did.

A cooperative, competency-based approach need not be clever. Often, there will be no obvious difference from many aspects of other programs. The differences are in attitude, "climate," and thinking. Beneath the inventive examples and suggestions I have been able to share from other programs is patience and persistence. Staff have been persistent in looking for success, in seeking to respond rather than react, and in trying (sometimes against enormous odds) to treat their clients as competent. They have been patient with each other (and with me, when I have had the opportunity to work with them) and patient with new ideas that do not show fruit overnight. When they have been clever, this has been a by-product of their persistence.

None of the examples of ideas will apply directly to your residential program. As with any therapy intervention, the most important criterion is that what you do in any particular situation *fits* with the context of your program.

The ideas in this book are not meant to be a comprehensive "framework" that can simply be applied to a residential program. As such, it is not a "model." To finish where we began, I will repeat a paragraph from the book's introduction .

It would be nice if we could have a manual for how to do residential treatment. Unfortunately, it is not that simple. If we did have a manual, we would find lots of situations where it did not apply or did not provide answers. This book aims to be practical, but it is not a manual. I hope it is a book of ideas and one that inspires you to rethink how your residential program operates.

REFERENCES

Adams-Westcott, J., & Isenbart, D. (1990). Using rituals to empower family members who have experienced child sexual abuse. In M. Durrant & C. White (Eds.), *Ideas for therapy with sexual abuse*. Adelaide, Australia: Dulwich Centre Publications.

Bateson, G. (1979). *Mind and nature: A necessary unity*. London: Wildwood House.

Bateson, G., & Bateson, M. C. (1987). *Angels fear*. New York: Macmillan.

Cade, B. (1985). Stuckness, unpredictability and change. *The Australian and New Zealand Journal of Family Therapy, 6*, 9–15.

Cade, B. (1988). The art of neglecting children: Passing the responsibility back. *Family Therapy Case Studies, 3*(2), 27–34.

Cade, B. (1989). Over-responsibility and under-responsibility: Opposite sides of the coin. *A celebration of family therapy — 10th anniversary issue of The Journal of Family Therapy*, Spring, 103–121.

Cade, B., & O'Hanlon, W. H. (1993). *A brief guide to brief therapy*. New York: W. W. Norton.

Coles, D. (1986). Taking a temper apart. *Family Therapy Case Studies, 1*(1), 35–42.

de Shazer, S. (1988). *Clues: Investigating solutions in brief therapy*. New York: W. W. Norton.

de Shazer, S. (1991). *Putting difference to work*. New York: W. W. Norton.

de Shazer, S., Berg, I. K., Lipchik, E., Nunnally, E., Molnar, A., Gingerich, W., & Weiner-Davis, M. (1986). Brief therapy: Focused solution development. *Family Process, 25*(2), 207–222.

Durrant, M. (1985). Bowling out fears: Test victory for double description. *Dulwich Centre Review*, 17–27. (Reprinted in *The Journal of Family Therapy*, 1987, 9)

Durrant, M. (1987). Therapy with young people who have been victims of sexual assault. *Family Therapy Case Studies, 2*(1), 57–63.

193

Durrant, M. (1991). When is a model not a model?: Contextual residential care in context—a reply to Tyndale and Kaye. *The Australian and New Zealand Journal of Family Therapy, 12*(3), 122–125.

Durrant, M., & Coles, D. (1990). Michael White's cybernetic approach. In T. Todd & M. Selekman (Eds.), *Family therapy approaches with adolescent substance abusers* (pp. 135–175). Boston, MA: Allyn & Bacon.

Durrant, M., & Kowalski, K. (1990). Overcoming the effects of sexual abuse: Developing a self-perception of competence. In M. Durrant & C. White (Eds.), *Ideas for therapy with sexual abuse* (pp. 65–110). Adelaide, Australia: Dulwich Centre Publications.

Durrant, M., & Kowalski, K. (1993). Enhancing views of competence. In S. Friedman (Ed.), *The new language of change: Constructive collaboration in psychotherapy.* New York: Guilford.

Epston, D. (1991). I am a bear: Discovering discoveries. *Family Therapy Case Studies, 6*(1), 11–20.

Fisch, R.,Weakland, J. H., & Segal, L. (1982). *The tactics of change: Doing therapy briefly.* San Francisco, CA: Jossey-Bass.

Furman, B., & Ahola, T. (1992). *Solution talk.* New York: W. W. Norton.

Heath, A. W., & Ayers, T. C. (1991). MRI brief therapy with adolescent substance abusers. In T. Todd & M. Selekman (Eds.), *Family therapy approaches with adolescent substance abusers* (pp. 135–175). Boston, MA: Allyn & Bacon.

Heisenberg, W. (1958). *Physics and philosophy.* New York: Harper & Row.

Imber-Black, E., Roberts, J., & Whiting, R. (Eds.). (1988). *Rituals in families and family therapy.* New York: W. W. Norton.

Kelly, G. (1955). *The psychology of personal constructs.* New York: W. W. Norton.

Kelly, G. (1963). *A theory of personality.* New York: W. W. Norton.

Kinney, J., Haapala, D., & Booth, C. (1991). *Keeping families together: The Homebuilders' model.* New York: Aldine de Gruyter.

Kobak, R. R., & Waters, D. B. (1984). Family therapy as a rite of passage: Play's the thing. *Family Process, 23*(1), 89–100.

Lipchik, E. (1988). Interviewing with a constructive ear. *Dulwich Centre Newsletter, Winter,* 3–7.

Lustig, H. (1975). *The artistry of Milton H. Erickson* (videotape). Ardmore, PA.

Menses, G., & Durrant, M. (1986). Contextual residential care: Applying the principles of cybernetic therapy to the residential treatment of irresponsible adolescents and their familes. *Dulwich Centre Review,* 3–13 (republished *Journal of Strategic and Systemic Therapies,* Summer 1987, 6(2), 3–15, and *Residential Treatment of Children and Youth,* 1990, 7(3), 11–32)

Molnar, A., & Lindquist, B. (1989). *Changing problem behavior in schools.* San Francisco, CA: Jossey-Bass.

O'Hanlon, W. H. (1990). A grand unified theory for brief therapy: Putting problems in context. In J. K. Zeig & S. G. Gilligan (Eds.), *Brief therapy: Myths, methods and metaphors* (pp. 78–89). New York: Brunner/Mazel.

O'Hanlon, W. H. (1993). Possibility therapy. In S. Gilligan & R. Price (Eds.), *Therapeutic conversations.* New York: W. W. Norton.

O'Hanlon, B., & Wilk, J. (1987). *Shifting contexts: The generation of effective psychotherapy.* New York: Guilford.

O'Hanlon, W. H., & Weiner-Davis, M. (1989). *In search of solutions: A new direction in psychotherapy.* New York: W. W. Norton.

Papp, P. (1988). Foreward. In E. Imber-Black, J. Roberts, & R. Whiting (Eds.), *Rituals in families and family therapy*. New York: W. W. Norton.

Roberts, J. (1988). Setting the frame: Definition, functions and typology of rituals. In E. Imber-Black, J. Roberts, & R. Whiting (Eds.), *Rituals in families and family therapy*. New York: W. W. Norton.

Rosenhan, D. L. (1973). On being sane in insane places. *Science, 179*(19 January), 250–258.

Rosenhan, D. L. (1975). The contextual nature of psychiatric diagnosis. *Journal of Abnormal Psychology, 84*(5), 462–474.

Simes, D., & Trotter, C. (1990). Tough boys discover choices: Dealing with violence in the residential care setting. *Family Therapy Case Studies, 5*(1), 51–60.

Tyndale, R., & Kaye, J. (1991). Contextual residential care reviewed. *The Australian and New Zealand Journal of Family Therapy, 12*(3), 117–121.

van Gennep, A. (1908). *The rites of passage*. London: Routledge & Kegan Paul.

Walter, J., & Peller, J. (1992). *Becoming solution-focused in brief therapy*. New York: Brunner/Mazel.

Watzlawick, P. (Ed.). (1984). *The invented reality*. New York: W. W. Norton.

Watzlawick, P.,Weakland, J. H., & Fisch, R. (1974). *Change: Principles of problem formation and problem resolution*. New York: W. W. Norton.

Weakland, J. H., Fisch, R.,Watzlawick, P., & Bodin, A. (1974). Brief therapy: Focused problem resolution. *Family Process, 13*(2), 141–168.

White, M. (1984). Pseudo encopresis: From avalanche to victory; From vicious to virtuous cycles. *Family Systems Medicine, 2*(2), 150–160.

White, M. (1986). Negative explanation, restraint and double description: A template for family therapy. *Family Process, 25*(2), 169–184.

White, M. (1989). The externalizing of the problem and the re-authoring of lives and relationships. *Dulwich Centre Newsletter, Summer*, 3–21.

White, M., & Epston, D. (1990). *Narrative means to therapeutic ends*. New York: W. W. Norton.

Zukav, G. (1979). *The dancing Wu-Li Masters: An overview of the new physics*. London: Fontana Paperbacks.

INDEX

197